WINNING

The Answers

WINNING

The Answers

CONFRONTING 74 OF THE TOUGHEST
QUESTIONS IN BUSINESS TODAY

Jack &
Suzy Welch

Collins

An Imprint of HarperCollinsPublishers

FIRST EDITION

Library of Congress Cataloging-in-Publication Data.
Welch, Jack, 1935–
    Winning : the answers : confronting 74 of the toughest questions
in business today / Jack Welch & Suzy Welch.
        p.   cm.
    The authors interpret, extend, and illustrate the ideas first out-
lined in their earlier book, Winning (©2005), through questions and
answers drawn from their column, "The Welch way," in the Friday
issues of BusinessWeek, from their book tour, and from speeches
and classroom discussions.
    ISBN-13: 978-0-06-124149-9
    ISBN-10: 0-06-124149-0
    1. Success in business.   2. Globalization—Economic aspects.
3. Industrial management.   4. Career development.
5. Organizational behavior.   I. Welch, Suzy.   II. Title.
    HF5386.W386   2007
    658.4'09—dc22   2006047249

06 07 08 09 10 ❖/RRD 10 9 8 7 6 5 4 3 2 1

CONTENTS

MANAGEMENT PRINCIPLES
AND PRACTICES ▪ 93

On Running a Business to Win

CAREERS ■ 167

On Life, Liberty, and the Pursuit of a Promotion

PRIVATELY HELD ■ 223

On Working for the Family

WINNING AND LOSING ■ 235

On Why Business Is Good

INTRODUCTION

In April 2005, we published a book called *Winning*. To our minds, its purpose couldn't have been more straightforward: we wanted to codify our thinking about the myriad insightful, probing, and often urgent questions we had received while traveling around the world for three years, speaking to hundreds of thousands of people about their work, career, and life challenges. We wanted, basically, to write a book that was both a philosophical treatise on fundamental business principles and gritty how-to manual in one, and in doing so, pretty much wrap up what had felt like a great, extended conversation.

Little did we know that *Winning* wouldn't wrap up anything—just the opposite!

There was the book tour, of course, and you expect some action doing that—you're out looking for it! But along with the usual TV and radio appearances, we also visited thirty-seven business schools across the United States and in Europe, and spoke to more than one hundred business groups in cities around the world. *Winning*, we quickly discovered, wasn't the "Hmm, very

well then, thank you" summary event we had antici-
pated. It was a "Hey, wait a minute, what about—" kind
of affair.

Winning, in essence, proved to us once again that
people have an insatiable thirst to talk about work. They
want to understand it better, debate its every nuance,
and find a way to do it better. Even after the book tour
ended, the questions kept coming.

In the past year alone, we have heard several thousand questions. It is an understatement to say the topics
run the gamut. There is the very macro, as in, "How can
developed nations compete with China?" and "What is
the role of Wal-Mart in society?" And the very micro, as
in, "How do I overcome my fear of public speaking?"
and "How do I manage the team I was a part of—until
yesterday?" An IT manager in Michigan asked us about
the future of the European Union, and a CEO from New
Jersey asked us to list the most important characteristics
to look for when hiring a sales force. Hundreds of people
have asked about how to get ahead in their careers, dozens about surviving a difficult boss, and two about the
appropriate use of candor with elderly workers. We've
heard from scads of employees at family-owned companies frustrated with an incompetent aunt or cousin
at the helm, or otherwise at the end of their rope with
nepotism. In a letter filled with poignancy, a recent col-

lege graduate from South Africa asked us how to acquire self-confidence. She said she was starting from zero. In another filled with bittersweet reflection, a British correspondent asked us how he could regain his, which he'd lost after being fired for poor performance. Some letters have been amusing, like the one from the Indonesian manager who asked us how she could stop her team from explaining all their decisions with the excuse "It was gut instinct!" And others dead serious, like the one from the Milwaukee engineer who said, "The time has come for me to advise my grandchildren what to do with their lives. So, what is the next big thing out there?"

Indeed, there has been so much give-and-take since *Winning*'s publication that we've often been reminded of what a Dutch entrepreneur told us during a visit to Amsterdam in 2002. "Every day in life," she said, "there is a new question."

She was more right than we could have ever predicted!

About a year ago, we realized that we had actually fallen in love with the continuing conversation sparked by *Winning*. For two people who get a kick out of talking and meeting people, it was pure fun. But more than that, it was fascinating. With every new encounter, we learned what people—young, old, and in between—working in completely different kinds of businesses and in vastly different parts of the world, cared about most passion-ately. We learned that in Africa, for most people, it's about starting anew. People are desperate to find ways to launch companies and careers; they dream of break-ing out of the survivalist lifestyle. In more developed na-tions, the concerns more commonly come from deeply dug trenches, with questions like, "How do we take the nonsense out of the budgeting process?" and "What can we do to make our HR department more effective?"

The continuing conversations after *Winning* also pushed us to delve into our own thinking more deeply and to explore more than a few business and career is-sues that we hadn't included in the book. Both were mind-expanding activities, to say the least. And finally, opportunities to talk to global audiences that followed *Winning* allowed us to keep spreading a message we think isn't proclaimed nearly enough—that business is the great engine of society. It creates jobs, pays taxes, and opens up economic opportunity like no other insti-tution. Yes, government plays a huge supporting role—we couldn't live in a civilized world without its services. But with its ability to provide for families, build careers, and give back, business, we believe, is the foundation of a thriving world.

And so, in September 2005, we took the New York Times Syndicate up on an invitation and started to write a weekly Q & A column that now appears in forty newspapers in countries around the world, from England and Japan, to South Africa and Mexico, to Sri Lanka and Bulgaria. In the United States, the column appears every Friday on the back page of *Business Week* magazine.

The book you now hold in your hands draws on the questions to our weekly columns, but also includes questions from our book tour, as well as questions we have received during recent speeches and classroom discussions. (We both now teach, Jack at MIT's Sloan School of Management and Suzy at Babson College's Center for Women's Leadership.) In general, all these questions fall into three categories.

The first is questions about the ideas that originally appeared in *Winning*, but with a twist—or a shove. For instance, many people have told us they agree with *Winning*'s message that candor makes business (and life) immensely better, but they cannot understand how it can be implemented in various situations, such as the polite cultures of Asia. Similarly, hundreds of people have written us about *Winning*'s case for differentiation, the ranking of employees into the top 20 percent of performers, the middle 70, and the bottom 10. Good idea, many said, but how can differentiation possibly be implemented at small companies, or growing companies, or sinking companies, or family companies, or Swedish companies, or you-name-it companies? (All possible, we said, as you'll see.)

The second category includes questions on topics not covered in *Winning* itself. These mainly coalesce around entrepreneurship and family business, but there are also questions about work and career situations so specific it didn't dawn on us to include them. One of our favorites is from a secretary who, after getting her MBA at night, still finds her company won't promote her. This entirely common problem of "embedded reputation" should have been in *Winning*. It's here instead. Thanks to questions from readers around the world, we also get a chance in this book to write about the important topics of what really motivates people, the challenge of suddenly becoming the boss of your former peers, and the three performance measurements we think make the most sense for general managers.

The final category of questions in this book concerns current events. With their long lead times, books in general do not tackle breaking news, and *Winning* was no exception. Our columns have allowed us to do that, with some incendiary results. Indeed, the questions (or, should we say, the answers!) in this book that have sparked the most debate are those we wrote on why women don't become CEOs more often, Wal-Mart's role in society, and the Enron verdict. With the first of these, we received numerous e-mails, most of them very thoughtful, about our assertion that women's careers are changed, not necessarily for the worse, by biology, i.e., having babies. The reaction was not nearly so civilized when we wrote about what we consider Wal-Mart's positive impact on the world. Yes, 65 percent of the letters that poured in supported the giant retailer and bemoaned its regular beating in the media. But the rest lambasted us and thoroughly decried the company as a destroyer of communities. Finally, much to our chagrin, our Enron answer was met with general negativity. We'd said the company was a rare case of corporate malfeasance. Dozens of e-mails from around the world made the case otherwise.

A word on how this book is organized, which is not by the three categories just outlined! Instead, to help you navigate targeted areas of interest, it is organized by subject matter. Every question we receive is unique, of course, but that said, many do fall into topical buckets. That is why one section of this book includes the best, most representative questions we have received about global competition, another focuses on working in a family business environment, and another on leadership. In all, there are six sections, about as wide-ranging in their scope as business itself.

This book, incidentally, features seventy-four questions and answers. There could have been more, but we've learned that it would be folly to try to be all-inclusive in any book about work. The questions that follow cover dozens of important topics, and perhaps every topic that is important to you.

But they do not cover everything.

Like life, the conversation about work will go on and on. It has to. Economies rise and fall. Competitive dynamics never stop changing. Careers zig and zag. And so, questions will keep coming.

We look forward to listening to them all.

GLOBAL COMPETITION

▪ *On the Brave New World* ▪

When we wrote *Winning*, we assumed that globalization had so incontrovertibly arrived that people were past resisting it and had moved on to vigorous adaptation. We were partially right. Most people do now grasp globalization's opportunities, such as expanding markets, but many still struggle with the other side of the equation—that is, how to combat "the fast-moving global competitors," as one exasperated manager put it, "popping up everywhere."

And pop up they will from here on out. With the emergence of India and China, and the gradual reawakening of Europe, the global economic system will only become more integrated. And as the answers that follow suggest, companies can't really delay. You have to get in the game now.

TAKING ON CHINA...AND EVERYONE ELSE

You've said that it is necessary to reduce costs by 30 to 40 percent to compete with China, with its negligible wages and undervalued currency. But how can you prevent the Chinese from then copying whatever method you come up with to achieve your goal?

—NEWCASTLE UPON TYNE, ENGLAND

You can't! You can't prevent the Chinese from copying any of your efficiency-boosting processes, and guess what, you can't prevent the Romanians, Mexicans, or the Americans, either. In fact, you have to assume that every one of your competitors, from Indonesia to Ireland, is eager and able to imitate your best practices. And that they will.

Which is why your question is worrisome. It sounds as if you might be getting that no-option-but-surrender feeling about today's competitive environment. But such defeatism kills companies. Instead, you have to get yourself energized by the challenge of finding breakthrough ideas and processes. Today's competitive dynamic has to make you want to run faster, think bigger, and work smarter.

And to what end? The answer is simple: innovation. There are, of course, other ways to compete, but without doubt, innovation is the most sustainable in today's global marketplace.

Luckily, there are two ways to innovate, and together they can deliver a real knockout punch.

The first form of innovation is exactly what you would expect: the discovery of something original and useful—a new molecule, a breakthrough piece of software, a game-changing technology. This kind of classic innovation, of course, can happen by accident (in a garage, say), but far more often, it occurs when companies actively build a culture where new ideas are celebrated and rewarded. It happens, in fact, when companies basically define themselves as laboratories for new products or services. Think of Procter & Gamble and Apple. Both epitomize the innovation culture—and its competitive advantages.

But there is a second, less glorified way of innovation that is just as effective. It is the continuous, aggressive improvement of what you already sell or how you already do business. Yes, people must innovate by discovering totally new concepts, as we've just described. But companies can (and must!) also innovate by searching for best practices, adapting them, and *continuously improving them.* It is that activity, in particular around costs, quality, and service, which will most effectively drive the 30 to 40 percent cost reductions required in today's competitive environment.

The process of continuous improvement really has no boundaries or limits. It is an R & D team finding a new way to make a long-established molecule do something different, and a software engineer finding new applications for an upgraded piece of old software. It is people throughout the organization pushing relentlessly to take established products and services to the next level, blowing up the status quo of "that's how it's done around here," and replacing it with a mind-set that shouts, "We are never done looking for a better way."

A best-practices culture, in other words, has no end-point. Once a company thinks it has left the competition somewhere in the dust, it needs to start searching again for the "new and improved," always staying one or two steps ahead.

If the search is continuous, it also has to be as wide as you can make it. Don't just seek out best practices hiding under a rock in your own backyard, that is, down the hall in another department or a hundred miles away in another division. Look at other companies in your industry—and outside too. GE learned the nitty-gritty of lean manufacturing by visiting Toyota factories around the world. It learned the art and science of improving inventory turns by studying best practices at American Standard, a plumbing and air-conditioning company. In fact, if there is one thing you can be sure of, it is that companies—if they are not direct competitors, of course—love to share success stories. They are proud to showcase what they are doing well. All you have to do is ask. And ask is what people in best-practices cultures do—all the time.

At this point, perhaps, you are thinking that it is easy to extol the virtues of a best-practices culture but much harder to put one in place. You are absolutely right. Too often, companies resort to sloganeering on this front. They give best practices the old motherhood and apple pie treatment. *Best practices are good,* they say, *we believe in best practices,* and so on. Of course, this kind of generic cheerleading results in...nothing.

In real best-practices cultures, the fanatic pursuit of new ideas is baked into the mission of the company. Moreover, searching for best practices and the desire to continuously learn and improve are behaviors that are evaluated in every performance appraisal and rewarded financially. In best-practices cultures, leaders hire and promote only people who have a thirst for continuous learning.

Without doubt, putting an innovation culture in place is hard. But doing so is not one of those choices you can sit around and debate. Either you buy into discovery plus continuous, never-ending improvement as a way of life in your company, or you can wave at your competitors—as they pass you by.

■   ■   ■

2

IS CHINA FOR EVERYONE?

We are a successful Canadian company whose two main competitors have just moved aggressively into China. We know they're losing money there. But still I worry that we're making a mistake by staying local— should I?

—ONTARIO, CANADA

Actually, don't just worry. Be afraid—be very afraid.

In a global world, scale is a competitive weapon you cannot ignore. And scale is what China can give you, with its vast markets, low-cost manufacturing, and increasingly strong technical talent. No wonder companies from around the world, including, it seems, your two main competitors, are tripping over themselves to get a foothold there.

It is also no surprise that your competitors, in their early efforts, are not yet profitable in China. Most foreign companies haven't yet figured out how to take the pain out of entry there. Regardless, even if your competitors appear to be in that category, remain paranoid. Because if they eventually do find a way to take advantage of China's opportunities, they could leap into another competitive league, leaving you far behind.

So, our first advice is to channel the energy you spend worrying to ask yourself a number of hard questions about *why* your competitors have gone to China. What exactly do they see? Is it just the huge market? Or do they have a unique product or service offering the Chinese will jump at? Is it a manufacturing cost edge, or is it a low-cost, low-investment process that will change the game? Is it access to new technologies that might change your product's functionality or design appeal to customers? Is it potential partnerships with Asian companies that will, in due time, send imports of your product back to Canada and the rest of the world?

Throughout this soul-searching process, your operating assumption must be that your competitors know something about China's upside that your company does not.

Even though that may not end up being true.

The fact is: China is littered with the wrecks of companies that went to China just to go to China. They went, for instance, because their two main competitors had gone, and someone in the organization (like you, perhaps) couldn't get a good night's sleep because of it. They went because the "China or bust" mantra is invoked everywhere these days, from business school classrooms to boardrooms, all duly reported in the media. They went because, well, there is just a pervasive sense that *everyone* is going.

None of these are good enough reasons.

Yes, the allure of China's scale is enormous, and the competitive power of scale is real. But there is no point going to China if you don't know how China's scale is going to make you a better, more productive, more profitable company. In that way, the decision to go to China is just like the decision to enter any new market, be it over a state line or across an ocean. It has to make strategic and financial sense. Maybe not immediately, but in a reasonable amount of time.

So, our final advice to you is where we started—that you should indeed worry. In fact, you should assume that your competitors have figured out how China's scale will improve their market position and economics going forward. Then take that fear and use it to start a conversation in your company about why you haven't figured out your company's China advantage.

It could be that there isn't one. Not every company has to go to China, but most do and most should.

As long as they know why.

■   ■   ■

3

REGARDING RUSSIA

Everybody's so excited about China. My company recently signed a joint venture there, but we're also thinking of moving into Russia. What do you think about its potential?

—CHARLOTTE, NORTH CAROLINA

Your comfort level with doing business in Russia depends on how much stomach and capacity you have for risk. Russia has huge potential for opportunity but plenty for disappointment too. You could say the same thing about China, perhaps, but it seems to us that by comparison, Russia has less upside and more obvious downside.

To start with, let's look at what's promising about Russia. Sure, it's a fraction of China's size, with China's one billion head count, but with 140 million people, Russia is bigger than every single-country market in Europe, not to mention Japan.

And without doubt, some sort of economic transformation is occurring in Russia. GDP growth has averaged more than 6 percent per year for the past six years. Compare that to France or Germany! Meanwhile, over the last five years, capital spending has averaged annual gains of greater than 10 percent, and personal income 12 percent.

The driver of all this growth has been Russia's enormous store of natural resources—timber, minerals, and most of all, oil. In fact, Russia has enough oil to make itself not only energy self-sufficient, but a significant exporter as well.

The Russia picture darkens, however, when you look at other facts. Something like a quarter of Russia's economy is underground, riddled with corruption, and impervious to any kind of regulation that makes business fair and transparent. We have long railed against regulation as a hallmark of bureaucracy, but for an outside investor, Russia makes a compelling case for the opposite view. You can really come to love regulation when you try to do business in a country that doesn't have any.

Russia, of course, doesn't have a lock on lawlessness. China has a veritable army of pirates, and many foreign companies trying to do business there have been stymied (or worse) by what we would consider blatant violations

of intellectual property law. Chinese lawlessness, however, is somewhat surreptitious compared to Russia's,
which we would take as a (small) sign that it is less ac-
cepted by officialdom.

Two more points of comparison about Russia and
China bear quick mention. The first is manufacturing.
China's is thriving. Russia's factories remain stuck in a
state of grim Communist-era disrepair. There just hasn't
been significant investment in bringing these facilities
into the twenty-first century. Meanwhile in China, new
factories are being built with an eye toward the future.

The second is social stratification. Russia is cash
rich—that oil!—but its distribution of wealth is a throw-
back to the days of the czars. A tiny number of people
have a ton of money; most people, especially those in the
vast countryside, have very little. There is virtually no
in-between. China, by contrast, has a growing consumer
base of more than one hundred million people—almost
as large as Russia's total population. Their purchasing
power will increasingly be able to support a healthy, sustainable economy.

Now, we don't want to sound too pessimistic about
Russia and too bullish on China. Both countries are in
the midst of grand experiments. Russia is trying to create
some mix of capitalism and democracy while using a to-

talitarian approach to fighting both general lawlessness and the scourge of terrorism. China is trying to create a form of society with no antecedent: a market-driven (i.e., free) economy within a Communist superstructure that limits personal freedom. Who knows where either of these works in progress will end up ten years from now, let alone fifty.

But when you come right down to it, China does have an edge for outside investors. Its population is bigger by almost a factor of ten, for starters. Second, its culture is more entrepreneurial; in our experience, there are simply more people in China than in Russia who are energized to win, creative, fierce, and ambitious. Third, China provides a more attractive export base, given its broad manufacturing and technology capabilities. And finally, and perhaps most important, China is focused on the industries of the future—electronics, medical devices, and other forms of technology. After oil and other natural resources, Russia's major industries are machine building and metalworking. Those are more yesterday's stories.

All in all, that's why for us, it feels hard to get as excited about Russia as about China. Still, your company is not unwise to expand there. It could turn out to be very smart. Time will tell.

Time has already told with China. In today's global

marketplace, you *have* to be there. That's not true of Russia, even with its expanding economy. But if you have the resources to absorb the risk of doing business there, why not?

■   ■   ■

4

WHY PARIS BURNED

When we were in Paris one weekend in November 2005, the riots were raging, and they were raging stil when we left for Stockholm a few days later. It was there—in Sweden, where immigrants make up a fifth of the population, and about 40 percent of this group's younger adults are unemployed—that a journalist urgently asked us to comment on the fierce debate that erupted along with the violence:

What, she wanted to know, should the leaders of France do to stop the bleeding? And what should the leaders of other European nations do to make sure it doesn't start?

Our answer, very simply, was that European governments needed to work together with private enterprise to create jobs. Not make-believe jobs in civil service, but real jobs in new companies. This can be achieved, we said, through tax and employment laws that encourage and reward entrepreneurialism, risk taking, and investment.

You would have thought we'd called for the public

drowning of puppies and kittens. The journalist was apoplectic.

"You are *wrong!*" she said. "The way to solve this problem is for the government to give unemployed people more money and benefits. Why do you oppose that solution?"

We oppose that solution because it is not a solution.

Look, we may never know exactly what caused the riots in France, but we can be sure of one thing. People who believe their future holds upward mobility and financial security rarely set cars on fire. Riots are an expression of frustration and anger. They are the outcry of the desperate.

There will be much less chance of riots in Europe when its underclass has hope.

Hope comes from many things—freedom and dignity foremost among them. But hope also comes in large part from work that has meaning and *opportunity*. Which brings us back to jobs—real jobs.

Now, government jobs are all well and good. They must be, since one in five French people hold one, and a recent survey found that 76 percent of all French people aged fifteen to thirty consider civil service jobs "attractive."

But no country can have a perpetually stagnant economy and at the same time feed more and more people into the civil service while continuing to support a generous social system of health care and education, as is the case in most developed European nations. With everyone working in dead-end positions, who would be left to pay the taxes necessary to fund the machine?

The facts are, Europe needs jobs in the private sector, and it needs them in a big way. Consider this stunning statistic, reported recently in a *Wall Street Journal* op-ed piece by Joel Kotkin of the New America Foundation. Over the past thirty-five years, Kotkin wrote, the U.S. economy has created fifty-seven million new jobs. Europe—with a combined GDP about the same size as that of the United States—has created just four million.

Four million! What is going on?

What's going on are laws and regulations that make investment costly, to put it mildly. In countries like France and Germany, there are few tax incentives for risky investments. And employment laws make it so expensive to lay people off that companies are loath to hire people in the first place.

And what's also going on is a pervasive European attitude, which can be summed up in one phrase: severe risk-aversion. When we were in Germany not long ago, we met many businesspeople and talked about that country's economic situation. All agreed that balance sheets in Germany—and Europe in general—had never looked healthier. And despite what appeared to be political logjams, underneath it all, corporations were "restructuring" to make existing businesses more competitive. That's healthy—but in most cases not good for new jobs. But when we asked why cash-rich companies weren't investing in new ventures and pumping up their M & A activity, you could practically see the beads of sweat forming on foreheads around the room.

"Oh, no, no—we invested in Internet companies in the late nineties," one executive said, "and we lost a lot. We don't need or want that kind of mess again!"

With all due respect, we said, it's time to get over the trauma. Business is about managing risk—not running from it. The best thing about the Internet bubble is what business learned from it. Traditional venture capitalists see losses as just part of the process.

Later, a pension fund manager in Sweden defended the lack of investment on the part of European companies by pointing to the growth of private equity across Europe. Yes, that trend is happening, and it is a good thing, but far from sufficient.

Private equity provides a transfusion to a sick patient—frequently a laggard division bought out of a large company. The first part of the "cure" is often to *reduce* employment. Now, restructuring is very good for competitiveness. And it's also very good for the company's country, as a healthy company will contribute to tax receipts. But to be clear, if and when private equity ever creates jobs, the growth is rarely explosive and usually takes quite some time.

The kind of job growth that Europe needs must give people hope—that is, opportunity—and that can come only from new businesses, the kind that pop up in the United States every day.

They pop up for many reasons.

First, the government makes it easy for them. The tax laws put in place in the 1980s and enhanced by President George W. Bush encourage capital formation. And employment laws make a flexible workforce possible.

Second, the U.S. culture celebrates risk taking. Entrepreneurs are national heroes—people who start huge job-creating machines, like Bill Gates, Michael Dell, Steve Jobs, and a host of others. During the U.S. publicity tour for our book, *Winning*, we spoke with about twenty thousand newly minted MBAs at thirty-seven schools across the country. According to our (unscientific) estimate, some 20 percent of these students told us that they were planning on starting their own businesses.

By contrast, finding an entrepreneur in Old Europe— especially one young and fired up—is a rare event. (We have certainly encountered more of this breed in Eastern European countries like Slovakia and Hungary.)

Finally, the United States has vibrant capital markets. There are investors everywhere with money, looking for new ideas and the passionate entrepreneurs who go with them.

The U.S. business environment, while by no means perfect, offers a stark contrast to the one in Europe right now.

Now, some people say that as awful as the riots were in France, they are bound to stop. And they won't start elsewhere either. The reason they give is that Europe's slowing population growth will, in time, create employment opportunities for all.

Reality isn't so easy.

Employment opportunity in Europe will come when governments and companies work together to create work—real work—in the form of exciting new jobs. Tax and employment laws will have to change, as will other government policies. And attitudes will have to change too—toward risk taking. Companies will need to take the plunge and invest in new ventures. Entrepreneurs will need to come out of their caves and start building the future.

Yes, some new ventures will fail.

But many will win. And with them, so will Europe.

■   ■   ■

5

VIVE L'EUROPE—JUST NOT YET

People are always talking about the future of China and India, but where do you see Europe in five years' time?

—FARMINGTON HILLS, MICHIGAN

G iven everything happening in Europe—every economic, political, social, and demographic trend, not to mention one million French people taking to the streets to protest one little labor reform—it would be very easy to write the whole continent off as dead.

But Europe isn't done for, and it won't be either.

Now, without doubt, Europe has been treading water for the past ten years. In fact, as the rest of the world has rushed to globalize and become more competitive, Europe has just kept its head above the waves of change.

We don't mean *all* of Europe, of course. Two decades ago, the UK faced the reality of the emerging global marketplace and liberalized its economy to stay competitive.

And several countries in Eastern Europe, such as Hungary and Slovakia, have thrown off the shackles of Communism with effective pro-business reforms.

But the promising economic news coming out of these countries is dwarfed by the disturbing news coming out of France, Germany, and Italy. With their aversion to capital investment and risk taking, the three pillars of Old Europe are practically paralyzed by the arteriosclerosis of their welfare-state economies.

Consider a few statistics.

Over the past thirty-five years, according to Joel Kotkin of the New America Foundation, the U.S. economy has created fifty-seven million new jobs. In the same period, Europe—with a combined GDP about the same size as that of the United States—has created just four million (and most of those were in government). Meanwhile, the European unemployment rate hovers around 10 percent, double that of the United States.

Nor is Europe positioned to reap the gains of the growing science and technology sectors. R & D spending per capita in France, Germany, and Italy, for instance, is about half that of the United States. Demographic statistics are similarly bleak. France, Germany, and Italy all have shrinking populations that (naturally) are also aging.

Perhaps most worrisome of all, the continent seems

to be suffering from a collective bad mood. Asked, "How satisfied are you with your life?" by a Harris Interactive poll, around 18 percent of Europeans (from France, Germany, and Italy) answered "very," compared to 57 percent of Americans. Worse, these Europeans said they felt stuck in their rut. Asked, "How do you expect your personal situation to change in five years?" only a third predicted improvement. By contrast, two-thirds of Americans expect a better future.

So, if Europeans themselves seem ready to write an obituary for the continent's future, why aren't we?

Three main reasons.

The first is that Europe is simply too large and established an economy to collapse. Remember 1980? Japanese competition was going to put America out of business. The U.S. unemployment rate approached 10 percent, inflation was at 14, and the prime rate was more than 20. As with Europeans today, Americans back then were so morose, President Jimmy Carter declared the country in "malaise."

But too much was at stake for surrender. Americans elected a new president whose defining characteristic was optimism. He galvanized national pride (and defense-sector spending) by taking on Communism, and he reduced taxes and released the entrepreneurial spirit that revived the American economy.

Europe similarly has too much history, infrastructure, and promise to slide into nothingness. Its workforce, for instance, is among the most highly educated in the world. And while tepid, there are some signs of emerging discontent with the status quo. The quasi reformer Angela Merkel was elected chancellor in Germany. And the French government, hoping to spark job growth, did attempt to change an employment rule. That reform was shot down by protest, but at least the government took a swing at progress. It will again—by necessity.

The second reason is Europe's exciting new cadre of transformative business leaders: Carlos Ghosn of Renault and Nissan, Dieter Zetsche of Mercedes, and Klaus Kleinfeld of Siemens, to name just three. These individuals, and they are not alone, understand that their companies operate in a global world and are making the tough changes required to stay competitive.

And the final reason that Old Europe will survive is New Europe. The Eastern European nations, with their pro-business governments, are churning out a whole new generation of entrepreneurs who see opportunity everywhere and boundaries nowhere.

During our last trip to Warsaw, for example, we heard a businessman give a speech to about three hundred other Polish entrepreneurs. He shocked them by saying, "We are getting too expensive here. I want my company to be the outsourcer of Europe, so I'm putting all my new operations in Ukraine—and you should too!" After a collective gasp, the group, albeit small, was electrified with excitement. And that, we would suggest, says more about the future of Europe than an opinion poll of French, German, and Italian grousers.

So, where will Europe be in five years?

It won't be thriving. But it will be better. In fact, drawing on the energy of its new business leaders and entrepreneurs, and increasingly cleansed of the calcifying effects of the socialist system, Europe will be well on the road to a positive economic future that apparently—and sadly—many of its own people don't foresee today.

■   ■   ■

6

OUTSOURCING
IS FOREVER

How can we change things in the United States so we don't have to outsource to India and other countries anymore?

—ORLANDO, FLORIDA

We can't—and we shouldn't.

Look, the debate over outsourcing should be over by now. It was pretty much all about politics to begin with. The question now is not how do we stop outsourcing, but how do we use outsourcing to enhance competitiveness in what is, and forever will be, a global marketplace.

Of course, outsourcing has not been painless; layoffs really hurt. Still, they have to be seen as part of a broader picture, one in which outsourcing is not only integral to the world economy, but crucial to our own.

Integral because economies, by definition, respond

to consumer demands. People have come to expect the lowest price and the highest quality in one package. And companies can't deliver on that expectation without moving around the world to capture cost advantages and innovative minds.

As for the impact of all this on the United States, well, it's pretty hard to criticize. Since mid-2003, the American economy has grown about 20 percent. That's more than $2.2 trillion—equal to the size of the total economy of China. Seven million jobs have been added. Wage growth has accelerated from 1.5 percent in early 1994 to more than 4 percent in the last year.

Such statistics, you can be sure, mean that outsourcing's opponents, many of whom disappeared into the woodwork even before the 2004 election, will not be out there in the 2006 campaign. Those foes had predicted American technology jobs would migrate in hordes. In fact, tech jobs have increased 17 percent from the pre-bubble 1999 level. No wonder most politicians now tout the overall benefits of an integrated global system.

If there is a problem with the U.S. economy right now, it is not the loss of jobs because of outsourcing. It is the shortage of skilled labor because of immigration restrictions. Indeed, if Congress really wanted to make our economy more competitive, it would be to raise the limits on H-1B visas, making it easier for educated foreigners to work here. Ideally, the whole program could be replaced by a permanent green card system that would draw skilled workers into a more positive, long-term relationship with the American culture—and ultimately build a better economic future for all of us.

So, to your question then, forget outsourcing. America's labor challenge today is talent insourcing.

■   ■   ■

7

GETTING GLOBAL BEFORE IT GETS YOU

How should a traditional company—with its solid structures, rigid processes, and long-term employees—change in order to compete with the fast-moving global competitors popping up everywhere?

—SÃO PAULO, BRAZIL

First, we're going to make an assumption. Your company is not under siege from global competitors quite yet. You're too calm.

That's OK, for now. But get ready, because the fact that "war" hasn't officially broken out will make your job going forward much more difficult than if your company was in well-publicized trouble. Organizational transformations, especially the brave-new-world kind required by global competition, almost never happen unless people really feel the need for it. Survival is a mighty motivator.

Without a crisis, oh, how people like the way things

are. A bureaucracy like yours, in fact, can feel like a warm bath. People never want to get out. And they certainly don't have an iota of desire to jump into ice water, which is how the radically different behaviors required by global competition will feel at first. After all, globally competitive organizations must be flat, fast, and transparent. Informal, candid communication is a must. And so too is a mind-set that has people constantly seeking best practices inside and outside the company.

Since people won't jump into ice water, they need a push. Which is why you, or any leader trying to galvanize change, has to make a case—and make it personal. Your people will change when, and only when, they see how new behaviors will improve the company and, more important, their own lives.

So, get gritty and detailed. Use as much data as you can gather on industry dynamics, profit margins, emerging technologies, political trends—whatever—to come up with two vivid story lines, one about what the company will become if it doesn't change and the other if it does. Contrast plant closings with growth opportunities at home and abroad, lost jobs with more interesting work, and flat or shrinking wages with more money for everyone.

Then start campaigning. Talk and talk and talk. Not believing—or absorbing—a tough message the first or second time around is just human nature. You will have to repeat your case to the point of gagging, and then repeat it again.

Eventually, however, if your case is compelling enough, behaviors will change. They will change faster if you publicly praise and celebrate them whenever they occur, and faster still if you reward the people who demonstrate them.

Speaking of people, two other actions will help your transformation effort into a company up to the challenges of a boundaryless marketplace. First, make sure you start to hire and promote only true believers—people who completely accept the case for change and will proselytize for it too. And second, make sure you start to ease out resisters who cannot let go of the good old days, no matter how much persuading they hear. Yes, some of these individuals may do their jobs satisfactorily, but they should be working someplace else.

That is, at one of the few companies left out there with no global competition.

■ ■ ■

8

THE HOME FIELD ADVANTAGE

Ever since the Czech Republic and other post-Communist countries have opened to outside investment, many foreign companies—in particular American and European ones—have mainly sent in their own people to run operations. The problem is that these managers are usually incompetent and bush league, and have only one skill, an ability to speak the mother tongue. They add nothing and end up relying on the innate loyalty and enthusiasm of local employees to get things done. Why are companies so foolish this way?

—PRAGUE, CZECH REPUBLIC

They're not foolish—they're just uneasy. Like American tourists who eat at the McDonald's on the Champs-Elysées or French tourists who bring their own wine into Disney World, they'd rather have comfort than authenticity. Now, preferring the familiar may not be a principle of great management, but it's certainly part of human behavior.

And look, the problem you describe is universal. It is not unique to American and European companies moving into the post-Communist world. From the beginning of modern globalization, companies have tended to "stick with their own kind" when opening up foreign operations. When the Japanese first moved into the United States, or anywhere else for that matter, they typically installed Japanese bosses. And the same pattern is true of the Germans, the British, and many other nationalities. They all want their own trusted people in charge of far-flung operations, especially at the beginning, when so much is unknown about the local environment.

The key phrase here is "at the beginning," because trouble of the type you describe begins when foreign companies stay in comfort mode and keep their own people in charge for longer than a few years. This tactic misses a real opportunity. Why? Because local people *always* know their own country better; they know how its government works and how its people think. They know which local universities produce the best minds; they can understand what people on TV, in living rooms, in bars, and on the factory floor are really saying about the country's political and economic future. They can always "work the system" with more insight and ease. And that's why good companies know that the sooner you put local executives in charge of foreign operations the better. And the best companies work hard from the day they arrive to find and develop local talent with global training programs, creating a pipeline chock-full of middle managers with a shot at the top.

Without doubt, there will always be global companies that don't move quickly enough to turn management over to local executives. But eventually, these companies will suffer from real brain drain, as smarter companies move in and steal the local talent for their own expanding operations. In thriving Eastern Europe, as in Asia, the competition for professional management is fierce. No foreign company can afford to keep local employees in lower-level positions, beneath the controlling cloak of executives from the motherland. The local talent will leave for companies that offer growth and a future, taking their knowledge with them.

So, while we understand your frustration with the "foolish" companies in your region who continue to value the devil they know over a leap into the unknown, don't worry too much. This problem is typically self-correcting. In time, good companies put local managers in charge. They have to.

■   ■   ■

LEADERSHIP

▪ *On Being a Better Boss* ▪

Y ou know the stereotype of the know-it-all boss who rules his people like an arrogant little dictator? There is probably some truth to it—and it probably happens at too many companies—but to read the e-mail questions and comments we receive is to see just how many people positively yearn to be great leaders. They want to reach into their people's minds and hearts to help them grow and thrive. They want to build trust, earn respect, and unleash their team's energy to win. Indeed, their passion can be best summarized by a South African engineer who e-mailed us the day he was promoted to manager for the first time. "My goal," he said, "is to be remembered by my team as the very best boss they ever had."

In one way or another, that's what every question—and answer—in this chapter is about.

9

ARE LEADERS BORN OR MADE?

Is it possible to train people to be effective leaders—or do you think that the best leaders are just born that way?

—BRASILIA, BRAZIL

For some people, the question of whether leaders are born or made is truly intellectual—fodder for a good classroom or dinner party debate. But for people like you, in front-line positions to hire, promote, and fire, the question "Who has the right stuff to lead?" definitely has more urgency. Getting the answer right can drive an organization's culture and performance to new levels. Getting it wrong can too—downward.

So, what's the answer? Of course, since we're talking about real life here, it isn't neat or simple. The fact is, some leadership traits *are* inborn, and they're whoppers. They matter a lot. On the other hand, two key leadership traits can be developed with training and experience—in fact, they need to be.

Before going any further, though, let's talk about our definition of leadership. It's comprised of five essential traits. These traits, by the way, do not include integrity, which is a requirement in any leadership position, or intelligence, which is likewise a ticket to the game in today's complex global marketplace. Nor do they include emotional maturity, another necessity. These three characteristics are baseline—they're givens.

So, let's go beyond them. From our experience, the first essential trait of leadership is positive energy—the capacity to go-go-go with healthy vigor and an upbeat attitude through good times and bad. The second is the ability to energize others, releasing *their* positive energy, to take any hill. The third trait is edge—the ability to make tough calls, to say yes or no, not maybe. The fourth trait is the talent to execute—very simply, get things done. Fifth and finally, leaders have passion. They care deeply. They sweat; they believe.

As you may have figured, positive energy and the ability to energize are pretty hardwired. They're basically personality. Similarly, passion feels inborn. Some people just seem to come fully loaded with intensity and curiosity; they naturally love people, life, and work. It's *in* them. It *is* them.

Edge and the ability to execute are different. New hires rarely show up with them in polished form, and even middle managers benefit from training in both. But the best teacher for these two traits is trench warfare. That's because edge and execution are largely a function of self-confidence. You can say yes or no a heck of a lot better when you've done it a bunch of times and seen how well decisiveness works. Likewise, only in real-world challenges can managers truly feel the power of moving quickly, demanding accountability, and rewarding results. They can also experience how damaging it is not to execute—a mistake most effective leaders don't make twice.

So, are leaders born or made? The answer (perhaps not surprisingly) is both. Your best strategy, then, is to hire for energy, the ability to energize, and passion. Go full force in training and developing edge and execution. Promote the people who have a good dose of all five traits. Always remember, though, that not everyone was meant to be a leader. But as long as you are one yourself—and you are—it's your job to find and build those who can be.

■   ■   ■

10

THE LEADERSHIP MIND-SET

I would like your advice and assistance as I have been appointed to a leadership position for the first time. The position is quite senior and very challenging, and I need to know how to conduct myself and handle the role itself.

—RANDBURG, SOUTH AFRICA

First of all, kudos are in order. Not for getting promoted, though that's great, but because you seem to understand that becoming a leader means you will actually have to change how you act. Too often, people who are promoted to their first leadership position miss that point. And their failure to do so probably trips up careers more than any other reason.

The fact is, being a leader changes everything.

Before you are a leader, success is all about growing yourself. It's about *your* achievement. *Your* performance. *Your* individual contributions. It's about *you* raising your hand and *you* getting called on and *you* delivering the right answer.

When you become a leader, success is all about growing others. It's about making the people who work for you smarter, bigger, and bolder. Nothing you do anymore as an individual matters except how you nurture and support your team and help its members increase their self-confidence. Yes, you will get your share of attention from above—but only inasmuch as your team wins. Put another way: your success as a leader will come not from what you do every day, but from the reflected glory of your team's performance.

Now, that's a big transition—and no question, it's hard. Being a leader basically requires a whole new mind-set, one that is constantly *not* thinking, "How can I stand out?" but *is* thinking, "How can I help my people do their jobs better?" Sometimes that mind-set requires undoing a couple of decades of momentum! After all, you have probably spent your entire life—starting in grade school and continuing through your last job—as an individual contributor, excelling at "raising your hand." But the good news is, you were probably promoted because someone above you in the organization believes you have the stuff to make the leap from star player to successful coach.

But what does that leap actually involve? First and

foremost, actively mentoring your people. Give feedback at every opportunity—not just at annual or semiannual performance reviews. Talk to your people about their performance after meetings, presentations, or visits to clients. Make every significant event a teaching moment, discussing with them what you like about what they are doing and ways they can improve. And there's no need to sugarcoat your exchanges! Use total candor, which happens incidentally to be one of the defining characteristics of effective leaders.

Getting into the skin of your people is another way of growing others. Exude positive energy about life and the work that you are doing together, show optimism about the future, and care. Care passionately about each person's performance and progress. Your energy will energize those around you.

And through it all, never forget—you're a leader now. It's not about you anymore. It's about them.

■   ■   ■

11

TOUGH GUYS FINISH FIRST

Do tough bosses really get more out of their people? Of course they get short-term results—but do they really help a company win in the long run?

—MILAN, ITALY

Yes and yes. But what a loaded question!

Loaded because how you define *tough* matters a lot to the answer. And loaded too because how tough a boss seems may very well depend on your own performance.

Look, *tough* is a multilayered term that is open to discussion. But there can be little debate that top performers with great results tend to worry and complain a lot less about "tough" bosses than people struggling to meet expectations. That may sound tough itself, but it's reality.

Let's talk about the meaning of *tough* first.

Without doubt, there are tough bosses who are nothing more than bullying, power-drunk jerks, and they're brutal to work for. They callously push their people, take credit when things go right, point fingers when they don't, and generally go very stingy on praise and rewards. They can also be moody, political, manipulative, secretive, or outright mean, or all of the above. Now, as you say, sometimes these tough bosses get good results. But it's rarely for long. At any decent company, they are removed or they self-destruct, whichever comes first.

But bosses exist along a spectrum, and the tough, destroyer types we just described are at one far extreme. At the other end—and equally damaging to the business— are the "Is everyone happy?" variety. Yes, they may be enjoyable to work for—getting paid was never so easy!— but their spinelessness typically translates into mediocre results. Why? At least three basic sins are at work: these "nice" bosses treat everyone with the same gentle, loving wimpiness; they explain away misses without meting out consequences; and they change direction according to the needs and wishes of the last person in their office. In a word, they have no edge!

Somewhere between the two extremes—and probably much closer to the hard end than the soft—are bosses who define the notion of tough the right way, and because of that manage to get strong, long-term performance from their people. It is not too much to say that these kinds of bosses are actually the heroes of business, not the villains. They might not make everyone feel warm and fuzzy, but their good results create a healthy, fair work environment where people and the company prosper, job security for employees who perform well, and value for shareholders. What more could you want?

To these types of bosses, tough means *tough-minded*. They set clear, challenging goals. They connect those goals with specific performance expectations. They conduct frequent, rigorous performance reviews. They reward results accordingly, with the most praise and the highest bonuses going to the most effective contributors, and commensurate compensation levels down the line, ending with nothing for nonstarters. They are relentlessly candid, letting everyone know where they stand and how the business is doing. Every single day, *good* tough bosses stretch people. They ask for a lot and they expect to get it.

Does that make them hard to work for? Of course! But here's where individual performance comes into play. If you're up to the challenge, working for a tough boss can be incredibly energizing, as you achieve in ways you never thought you could. But if a tough boss raises the bar to a point that you are out of your league, then you're likely to hate the experience. And thanks to human nature, chances are you won't blame yourself— you'll blame the "tough" boss.

A perfect example of this dynamic in action is Bob Nardelli, CEO of The Home Depot, and a *good* tough boss—demanding, to be sure, but fair, transparent, and results focused.

In a recent *BusinessWeek* article lauding Bob's five-year turnaround at Home Depot, the usual "other side of the story" came in the form of complaints from former company executives, who claimed that Bob had created an oppressive "culture of fear" at the company. Note that these executives—none of whom agreed to be identified—no longer work at the company. You have to wonder why they left.

Was it because Bob was too "tough"?

Or was it because his tough-mindedness created performance standards they could not meet?

We bet on the latter. The point is: there are good tough bosses and bad ones, and which is which is often in the eye of the beholder.

Again, we're clearly not talking here about the egregious cases of jerk bosses who berate, belittle, and beat up their people. Everyone hates them, and they deserve their universal loathing.

We're talking about bosses who operate in the middle ground—bosses who are tough but fair, push hard but reward in equal measure, and who give it to you straight.

Weak performers usually wish these bosses would go away.

People who want to win seek them out.

■   ■   ■

12

THE ULTIMATE VALUES TEST

For the past two years, I have managed "Charles," who consistently delivers the numbers. He also alienates everyone by playing favorites, being arrogant, and acting secretive. Part of me wants to fire the guy. The other part can't imagine living without him. Your advice?

—GREAT NECK, NEW YORK

Confront him, and then fire him if he refuses to change. Because if you have ever opened your mouth at work and praised values like fairness, transparency, and information sharing, you have to. By stark contrast, to let Charles stay is to inform your employees that everything you say is meaningless drivel.

Look, if you want certain behaviors from your people, and you advocate for them as part of a winning approach to business and life, then you have to reward the people who demonstrate them.

Just as important, you have to get rid of the people who don't.

And this is key: don't get rid of "value offenders" surreptitiously with excuses like, "Charles left for personal reasons, to spend more time with his family." You need to stand up and publicly announce that Charles was asked to leave because he didn't adhere to specific company values.

You can be sure Charles's replacement will act differently, not to mention anyone else doubting your commitment to the values.

Now, obviously, every company wants people who deliver great results, like Charles. Your goal is to make sure your employees can do that and demonstrate good behaviors at the same time. No one should get ahead on the backs of other people. All that does is build an atmosphere of resentment and fear. Sure, you can win with that kind of culture—but not for very long.

So, grit your teeth and get rid of Charles. It might be painful for a minute, but you'll quickly be surprised by the increased effort—and improved results—you get from the rest of the team as a result of your decision to stand up and "walk the talk."

■ ■ ■

13

WHEN TO CUT THE CORD

As a small firm, we have plenty of typical start-up issues, like cash flow, but our real problem right now is "Mark," one of the managing directors, who just blew a major project and doesn't seem to understand the damage he's caused. My gut feeling is Mark should be fired, but his absence will, at least at first, hit us hard. Mark is a technical expert who's been with us from the start. Still, his poor management style and double agenda have reached an untenable level. Mark believes his decade of service and "loyalty" should protect him. I agree to a point, but believe performance matters more. What should we do?

—JOHANNESBURG, SOUTH AFRICA

Small companies really have a raw deal when it comes to letting people go. Big companies can carry turkeys for a long time; there are so many other people to cover for their mistakes. And when an underperformer *is* finally asked to leave a big company, he or she can usually slide out a side door without showstopping trauma to the individual, organization, or the work.

In small companies, by contrast, the blunders of bad performers usually hit the bottom line hard and fast. And just as bad, when it comes time to let them go, there is something that just feels so personal about it. A departure can feel like a death in the family. And that doesn't even take into account the impact on the work. Even if the fired employee was more bad than good, his removal can significantly affect operations, not to mention client relations.

Still, as you know in your bones, Mark has to go.

There are really only four kinds of managers in the world, classified by how well they perform—i.e., deliver results—and how well they demonstrate good values, such as candor and customer responsiveness. Managers who deliver great results and adhere to good values are easy. They should be praised and rewarded at every opportunity. Managers with poor results but good values deserve another chance, maybe in another position within the organization. The third kind of manager, with great results and lousy values is the kind that usually destroys organizations. They deliver the numbers, but usually on the backs of their people. Companies very often keep these jerks around for way too long, destroying morale and trust as they do. But that isn't even your problem.

With Mark, you have the easiest kind of manager to deal with. He's got poor performance and poor values. You mention, for instance, his "double agenda." Not only did he blow a major project, he's out for himself and playing politics. He's "loyal," he says. Doesn't sound that way.

Look, the game is over. You may very well miss Mark's technical expertise until a replacement can be found, but when you finally get the guts to cut the cord, you'll wonder why you didn't do it sooner.

14

THE COURAGE TO BECOME
A CHANGE AGENT

I am new to management, and eight months ago was made the head of a learning and development department, which has seven people, all of them older than I am and with more years of service to the company, a global natural resources business. I am overwhelmed by the poor work ethic among my staff. They frequently ask for time off for personal matters and have low productivity in general. How do I say no to repeated personal requests for time off if the company itself allows for flextime?

—CAPE TOWN, SOUTH AFRICA

We have a question for you. How much courage have *you* got, because you are going to need it in the difficult change campaign that awaits you. Difficult, because you need to turn your department upside down to get things right, and even when that's done, some people may still have to go.

You don't say so, but we would guess that your department is lacking three critical organizational components: an inspirational mission, a clear set of values, and a rigorous appraisal system. A mission will illuminate your department's overarching purpose and give your people a sense of excitement and urgency. A set of values will describe how people need to *act* in order to achieve the mission. (Another word for *values*, incidentally, is simply *behaviors*.) For instance, in a learning and development department like yours, the values might include "Connect all coursework to changing market conditions," or "Spread best practices to every corner of the company." Whatever—these are just examples of the kind of concreteness that makes values come alive. Finally, a candid, rigorous appraisal system (conducted at least twice a year to start) will let your people know how well they are delivering results and demonstrating the values. The appraisal system must differentiate, by the way, or it will be meaningless. In other words, it must result in praises, raises, and promotions for the people who buy into the new mission and values, and just the opposite for those who don't.

The change campaign we've just described is major

and disruptive, and it will take time and steel nerves, even in a small department like yours. But once a mission, a set of values, and an appraisal system are in place and relentlessly communicated by you, people will know what it takes to succeed. That, in and of itself, should decrease the frequent requests for personal time. How? By making it clear that time off is fine—as long it has been *earned* with good performance and the right values. Eventually, you should see an overall improved work ethic and higher productivity. That said, there are sure to be some people who can't change their ways, even with your encouragement and guidance. Don't wait too long; let them know they need to move on to an organization where their values are a better fit. They don't belong in yours.

Now, we realize you are part of a larger company with its own culture and practices. Indeed, that's often what we hear from people in your predicament—"I can't change things because that's not the way it's done here," they say, or, "The bosses won't support me."

We sympathize—but not totally. Yes, you may be an outlier, but in our experience, it is rare for an organization, *especially* its bosses, to reject a change initiative that improves performance and productivity. Very few people want to shoot a team member who is delivering results. They may be jealous, but they're not stupid.

But even if you are working within a company where your plan is "outside the box," don't give up. Just move more judiciously. Make sure the reasons for your change initiative are transparent to everyone. Keep your bosses informed of where you are going, and your team even more so. And finally, don't lose faith along the way. Some people will resist change. They always do. But as soon as results start rolling in, your new approach will make its own case, loud and clear.

■   ■   ■

15

WRESTLING WITH RESISTERS

For eight months, I have been running a company with enormous growth prospects, but now find myself facing a real barrier to progress. Certain members of my team, ten years older than me and with fifteen years seniority, are unwilling to change. In fact, it has taken me more than four months to get some of them to accept different ways of doing things. What should I do?

—MEXICO CITY, MEXICO

First off, you can slow down a bit. Four months is too short a time to convince most people to change their morning coffee routine, let alone how to do work they think they're very good at already.

But that doesn't mean you stop pushing for change. In fact, even as you recalibrate your timing, be certain you really have a "wow" vision of the future to sell your team. By "wow," we mean a vision that is inspirational from a business perspective, but as important, one that speaks to the real question on everyone's mind during any change program: "Hey, what's in this for me?" The answer could be increased job security, or more money, or better opportunities for promotions down the road— or all three. Just make sure that every time you mention the company's need for strategic change, you include a subtle (or not-so-subtle) message about the positive personal outcomes. Even if people are older and more senior, they will hear it.

And then, as soon as the change program's early wins start occurring, perhaps in the form of higher margins or more customers, deliver on your promises. That is, increase salaries, give extra bonuses, or promote people more quickly. Nothing overcomes resistance to change faster than success, especially if that success improves the lives and careers of the team who made it happen.

That said, there are simply some people who constitutionally cannot stomach change. You'll never be able to sell them your vision, convince them that there's something in it for them, or reward them enough when it occurs. Luckily, these diehard resisters are actually few in number. We figure that about 10 percent of employees are born "change agents," embracing the new with energy and optimism. Another 75 percent or so may not lead the charge, but once they are persuaded change is necessary, say, "OK already, let's get on with it." The re-

mainder are resisters, who are just so entrenched in the
the old way, either emotionally, intellectually, or politically, that they will fight change until the bitter end.

These people usually have to go. And when they do,
you have a big responsibility not to let them quietly depart "for personal reasons." That phony pabulum does
the organization no good whatsoever. When hard-core
resisters depart, you need to let everyone know they had
to leave because they did not buy into the new vision.
Yes, wish them well, and even help them find another
job where their approach fits. But don't pretend that
people who do not accept the future can stay in the fold.
They can't.

Most change programs usually take about a year
to get traction—that is, before people start to feel any
impact and know the change is for real. If you have a
persuasive case and lots of positive energy, most of your
team will come with you, even some of the "older and
wiser" ones who seem so resistant today.

■   ■   ■

16

BUILDING TRUST FROM THE TOP DOWN

Is there a short answer for building trust in the work-place?

—JOHANNESBURG, SOUTH AFRICA

Yes, very short: Say what you mean, and do what you say!

Trust fritters and dies two ways. First, when people aren't candid with one another. They sugarcoat tough messages. They use jargon and baloney to purposely make matters obscure and, therefore, themselves less accountable. The only way to get candor into an organization is for the bosses to identify it as a top value, consistently demonstrate it themselves, and reward those who follow their lead.

The second trust killer is when people say one thing and do another. Again, bosses are the main culprits. They tell people to take risks but excoriate them when they fail. They endorse stretch budgets and invite their people to dream big, but punish them if the numbers fall short, even at the end of a decent year. They proclaim a commitment to customer service, but let the factory ship less-than-perfect product to make the month's sales quota. Or perhaps worst of all, they espouse the company's values at the top of their lungs, but keep and reward people who don't live those values *simply because they make the numbers*. All that tells the organization is, nothing I say means anything. Or put another way: don't trust me.

Trust, ultimately, isn't very complicated. It's earned through words and actions—and integrity in both.

■   ■   ■

17

THE PERILOUS PROMOTION TRAP

For four years, I ran a single store in a large national retail chain, but I was recently promoted to oversee multiple stores across two states. I am finding, however, old habits hard to break—in particular, I still worry more about the performance of one store (my old one!) than what's going on at all my stores. Any advice?

—HUNTINGTON STATION, NEW YORK

You've nailed it—and bravo for that. Most people in your position don't have the self-confidence to realize that they have fallen into one of the most common traps of moving up, that is, excitedly taking on a new job but keeping one foot in the old.

The facts are, with your promotion, two people got new jobs: you and the person who replaced you. As a leader now, your task is to unleash the innovative new ideas *both* of you have. You can't do that—and neither can your replacement—if you are spending your energy "going home" all the time.

Instead, spend your energy getting to know your expanded new world—and raising the bar across it.

How?

Start by thinking of all your stores as laboratories. Yes, they all do roughly the same thing, but certainly some of them have unique methods or procedures that are more effective. Your job is to spot those best practices and champion them as if they were the best things since oxygen and hydrogen. In your new role, you want everyone in all your stores talking about one another's best ideas, adopting them, and improving them. That will add a lot more value than you looking over someone's shoulder.

Transparency is another great tool you can use to raise the bar. You already know which metrics drive performance in your business—inventory turns, sales per square foot, or some key measure of customer satisfaction. If those metrics aren't already disseminated on a regular basis, fix that right away. Make sure every store sees the comparative ratings, ranked from best to worst. Such clarity works wonders. It's a very motivating form of public recognition for top-performing stores, and it also signals to poor performers exactly where they can look for new and more effective approaches to the work. In other words, it supports and expedites continuous learning and improvement.

A final way to raise the bar and avoid the "foot in the old" trap is to move quickly to conduct regular, rigorous performance evaluations of *all* your managers. Your qualitative assessments will be based on how well people demonstrate the desired values (that is, behaviors) you have laid out—such as transferring and adopting good new ideas—and your quantitative assessment will be based on the transparent metrics system you're driving. The assessments together give you a real opportunity to reward and celebrate your best people, support and coach your middle group, and weed out underperformers. The outcome: higher performance standards for everyone.

Your new job is bigger than your old one, but more important, it is different. You've got a lot to do now, but it doesn't include what you used to do. Leave that to the person in your old office, who can get busy reinventing the "perfect situation" you left behind!

■ ■ ■

18

KEEPING YOUR PEOPLE PUMPED

In our business, the biggest challenge we have today is motivating our people. What's the best way to do that?

— GABORONE, BOTSWANA

Besides money, you mean?

We're assuming you do, because as a boss, you surely have seen how effective money is in lighting a motivational fire—even in your employees who claim that money really doesn't matter to them! Indeed, money's power to energize people is so tried-and-true we won't dwell on it. Nor will we talk about two other well-established motivators: interesting work content and enjoyable coworkers. You already know how effective these conditions are in getting your people to invest heart and soul in their jobs. Like money, they're motivational no-brainers.

But if three no-brainers were all that motivation took,

it wouldn't be, as you correctly note, the huge challenge it is.

So, what else can you do? Fortunately, there are four other motivational tools you can unleash, all nonmonetary and each very effective.

The first of them is easy: recognition. When an individual or a team does something notable, make a big deal of it. Announce it publicly, talk about it at every chance. Hand out awards.

Now, when we make this suggestion to business groups, almost inevitably someone expresses concern for the people *not* being recognized. They might be hurt, they say, or demotivated by such a display. This is nonsense; it's indulging the wrong crowd! If you have the right people in your company—that is, competitive and upbeat team players—public recognition only raises the bar for everyone.

One more note on recognition, in particular when it comes in the form of an engraved doodad. These types of items are all well and good, but remember, they can never be given in lieu of money. They are an addendum. Plaques gather dust; checks can be cashed.

The second tool should be easy, but apparently it's not: celebration. We say that because everywhere we go, we ask audiences if they think their companies celebrate success enough, and we typically get no more than 10 percent of the crowd saying yes. What a lost opportunity! Celebrating victories along the way is an amazingly effective way to keep people engaged in the whole journey. And we're not talking about celebrating just the big wins—we're talking about marking milestones like a big order or a new way of doing things that increases productivity or customer satisfaction. You name it—all these small successes are chances to congratulate the team and boost their spirits for the challenges ahead.

Celebrations don't need to be fancy or expensive; after all, a celebration is really just another form of recognition, but with more fun involved. It can be throwing a surprise barbecue one afternoon. It can be tickets to a ball game or a movie. It can be sending a couple of high performers and their families to Disney World, or the San Diego Zoo, or the Rose Bowl parade, or whatever happens to turn their crank.

Which brings us to what celebration is not. Celebration is not going out to dinner with you. Almost nothing strikes darkness in the hearts of employees more than a boss saying, "Great job! I'm taking everyone to Mama Maria's tonight!" Look, your people spend all day with you, and they may like you very much. But it is not motivating to be rewarded by a forced march to an after-hours affair, even if the food is great.

The next motivational tool is really powerful, but it can be used only if you're absolutely clear about your mission. Now, you may be thinking, "Aren't all bosses clear about the mission?" But too often they're not. In fact, in the course of our travels over the past several years, we've discovered that many leaders are so busy with the daily grind that their missions fall by the wayside.

It is inevitable, of course, that crises will divert attention from your mission on occasion, but to move forward, a team has to understand and buy into where it's going. It needs a shared goal, a collective sense of purpose. And that's exactly what a great mission gives you: a bold, inspirational creed to capture the hearts and souls of your people. A mission allows bosses to say, "There's the hill. Let's take it together!"—a motivating rallying cry if there ever was one.

The final motivational tool we'll mention here is probably the most difficult to implement. Yes, many great leaders have it as part of their "touch," but for those less seasoned, it's pretty hard to pull off.

We're talking about creating a work environment with just the right balance of achievement and challenge. People need a feeling of success to be excited about work. But they get bored if they are not being tested too—that is, if they are not learning and growing. In other words, people are motivated when they feel as if they are at the top of the mountain *and* as if they are still climbing it.

Simply put, bosses who create jobs with this kind of built-in push and pull have a real competitive advantage. Their people are motivated that extra degree, and it really shows in performance.

Now, back to money.

Of course there are people who aren't moved by financial rewards, but they rarely gravitate toward business careers. That's why when you think about motivation, you need to think about financial rewards first.

But remember, it's not always how much you give people, sometimes, it's how much you give them relative to their peers. We were recently talking with an investment banker we know well, and we asked him how his year went. He was obviously pleased with the amount of his bonus, but he was just as excited by how it measured up to the other top rainmakers in his firm. Money is a way of keeping score, and the question "Who's better or best?" seems to keep a lot of people stretching.

That said, even investment bankers (at least, some of them) care about more than money. In fact, very few good people will stay in a job where money is the *only* thing going for it. They want money plus a certain feeling—a feeling that they matter. Basically, people want to know that what they do eight hours a day, and usually much more, means something. Fortunately, you can show them that with open appreciation, a sense of fun, an exciting shared goal, and individual attention to the challenge of each job.

Those are a lot for any boss to give, but they're free and the returns incalculable.

■   ■   ■

19

HOW TO GET ELECTED BOSS

I was just promoted and will now become the manager of the team I once belonged to. Any advice on how to make a successful transition?

—FOLSOM, CALIFORNIA

Yes—start campaigning. The company's higher-ups have just appointed you boss. Congratulations. Now comes the hard part: you need to go out and get elected by your former peers.

And this part is not just hard, it's *very* hard. In fact, the transition from peer to manager is one of the most delicate and complicated organizational situations you will ever experience. For months or even years, you have been in the trenches with your coworkers as a friend, confidant, and (probably) fellow grouser. You've heard secrets and told a few. You know about every little feud and grudge. You've sat around in airport waiting rooms and at weekend barbecues with your closest colleagues

and ranked everyone else on the team. You've pontifi-
cated about who would go, who would stay, and generally what you would do if you ran the group.

And now you do.

Surely, some of your former peers are cheering your
promotion and are eager to fall in line. That will feel
very good to you, but don't let their support lead you to
do something disastrous—namely, come out of the gate
with guns blazing. No, keep them firmly in your holster.

Why? Because just as surely as some are cheering,
others are not. No matter how sure you are that you
are right for the job or how popular you once were as
a member of the team, some of your former peers are
uncomfortable with your promotion. A couple may have
wanted the job themselves and thought they deserved
it, so they're feeling anything from hurt to bitter. Others will simply have some level of anxiety about you
going from "one of us" to "one of them"—especially with
what you know, not to mention your opinions (known
or suspected) about certain people and the way things
are done. Either way, these former peers are in a holding
pattern right now, checking you out.

And that's where you should be too—in a holding pattern, checking *them* out. In fact, checking everything out.

Which is why you need to start campaigning, that is,

winning them over. You need to create an atmosphere of stability and cohesion where sound judgments about the future can be made—by everyone.

Look, the last thing you want in your new role is a revolution or an exodus or even low-level disgruntlement. You want people settled down and functioning. The reason is straightforward enough. When and if there are changes down the road, you want to make them on your terms.

In other words, you want to make changes amid strong buy-in from a team of engaged supporters—not despite the resistance or over the nattering of a confused or chaotic crew.

And by the way, it does nothing for your career or your political standing in an organization to launch into your new job with a period of turmoil. Much better to be known as a keeper of the peace who leaps into action only when the troops are prepared to fight for a mission they believe in.

And so, campaign you must.

But here's the rub: you have to do that without compromising your new authority. That's right: you have to run for office while holding office—and doing all the things an officeholder must do!

And there's your quandary—the hard part, as we said—the need for you to campaign and command simultaneously. That's what the transition from peer to manager is all about.

Getting it right is all about timing.

Your kinder, gentler election drive cannot last for-ever. In fact, give it three months—six at most. By that time, if you haven't won the vote of a former peer or two or three, you won't ever. In fact, after a certain point, the softer you are, the less effective you will become as you fight battles that do nothing but wear you down. So, save your energy and attention for bigger things, and begin the process of moving steadfast resisters out—and bringing in people who readily accept the changes that you and your new core of supporters see as necessary.

The fact is, running for office goes with the territory of being promoted, and all effective managers go through it—often, several times in their careers. Fortunately, the transition period does not last forever, and if you handle it right—with a campaign and not chaos—you'll be in a great position to do what's best for the organization and yourself.

Lead from strength.

■   ■   ■

20

WINNING THE WHINING GAME

I run a fourteen-person business, and we look after our people very well—parties for birthdays, babies, and marriages, and a real interest in each individual, both personally and professionally. Still, people complain incessantly. There's too much politics, not enough appreciation, and so on. I am about to tear my hair out because nothing seems to make them happy.

—CAPE TOWN, SOUTH AFRICA

Stop trying. With the best of intentions, you have created a classic entitlement culture, in which your people have the deal exactly backward. They think *you* work for *them*.

This phenomenon is not uncommon, although it tends to be more prevalent in small organizations, where employees can more easily develop casual, familial relationships with their bosses, and bosses more often blur professional lines themselves.

In the end, such cozy familiarity can backfire, as is happening with you and your moaning, groaning employees.

It's irrelevant, however, how you got yourself into your predicament. It only matters now that you get out quickly, and the first person you need to get straight with is yourself. You are running a company, not a social club or a counseling service. Your number one priority is to win in the marketplace so that you can continue to grow and provide opportunities for your people. Of course, you want your employees to be happy. But their happiness needs to come from the company's success, not from their every need being met. When the company does well because of their performance, they will thrive, personally and professionally. Not the other way around.

Consider this way of thinking your new creed.

Next, gather your people together, and let them know about your conversion experience, and your plan to convert them too. Together, you and your staff will need to create a list of behaviors that will result in the company's winning. These behaviors will become your new company values—guidelines, if you will, to live by. For instance, one value could be: we will respond with a sense of urgency to customer requests. Or, we will only ship products with zero defects. The point of this process is very simple: to help your people understand that work is about . . . well, it's about *work*.

Without doubt, you will hear yelps of pain as you dismantle your entitlement culture. Indeed, some employees that you like and value may leave in protest. Take the hit and wish them well.

They will soon find out the grass is not greener on the other side, and you will discover how much better your company operates when your main concern is not whining—but winning.

■   ■   ■

21

NEW JOB—OLD TEAM?

I have just been hired in a leadership position at a new company. I am tempted to bring along some people from my old organization; we work together well, and they have the skills. Your thoughts?

—BANGALORE, INDIA

A tempting idea but a tricky one. The answer is, in a phrase, it depends.

If you're running a company that requires a rapid turnaround in a changing environment, and you are saddled with an embedded culture of employees in a state of denial, you'd be smart to bring along capable former colleagues you'd trust in a foxhole. Together, you'll get the work done faster and more smoothly, and with the camaraderie born of your shared experiences in the past, it will be a lot more fun too.

But if you've been hired to lead a relatively good business that mainly needs a dose of reenergizing, hiring several members of your old team can create a lot of mayhem for very little gain. Nothing is more demotivating to a functioning organization than a little imported cabal that regularly invokes, "This is how we did it at our old company." In the worst-case scenario, this dynamic gives rise to a two-class society: the boss's favored insiders and the alienated has-beens.

Bottom line: survey the terrain. Bring in your old team only if you need fast change and resisters won't budge. If you're not in a crisis situation, search out the best among the team you've inherited, and give them a new sense of purpose. You may miss your former colleagues, but you sure won't miss the havoc they would cause.

■   ■   ■

22

THE SMARTER THEY ARE . . .

I am looking for advice about a situation you've probably had to deal with: a superior employee. You can't
fire yourself, so what's the solution? Do you keep a lid
on the employee's performance? Or hope the organization doesn't figure out your underling is better than you
are?

—ORANGE, CALIFORNIA

Or how about this: you celebrate.

Look, the best thing that can happen to you as a
boss—and you're right, it has happened to both of us—
is hiring a person who is smarter, more creative, or in
some way more talented than you are. It's like winning
the lottery. Suddenly, you've got a team member whose
talent will very likely improve everyone's performance
and reputation.

Including yours.

Yes, it's human nature to feel as you do—fearful that

a "superior" employee could make you look, well, infe-
rior, and perhaps slow down your career progress. But in
reality, the exact opposite usually occurs.

The reason is that leaders are generally not judged
on their personal output. What would be the point of
evaluating them like individual contributors? Rather,
most leaders are judged on how well they've hired,
coached, and motivated their people, individually and
collectively—all of which shows up in the results. That's
why when you sign up top performers and release their
energy, you don't look bad. You look like the goose that
laid the golden egg.

So, keep laying them. It is a rare company that doesn't
love a boss who finds great people and creates an environment where they flourish, and you don't have to be
the smartest person in the room to do that. Indeed, when
you consistently demonstrate that leadership skill, and
come to be known as the person in your company who
can land and build the best, watch your career take off.

Now, we're not saying that managing "superior" employees on your team is necessarily easy. Your question,
in fact, reminds us of one we received in Chicago several years ago from an audience member who said two
of his seven direct reports were smarter than he was, and
asked, "How can I possibly appraise them?"

"What the heck happened to the other five?" was

our attempt at a lighthearted response. But we took his point. How in the world do you evaluate people who you feel are more talented than you?

You don't. That is, you don't evaluate them on their intelligence or particular skill set. Of course, you talk about what they are doing well, but as important, you focus on areas in which they can improve. It is no secret that some very smart people have trouble, for instance, relating to colleagues or being open to other people's ideas. Indeed, some struggle with becoming leaders themselves. And that is where your experience and self-confidence come into play and your coaching can really help.

In that way, then, managing superior employees is just like managing regular types. You have everything to gain from celebrating their growth—and nothing at all to fear.

■   ■   ■

MANAGEMENT PRINCIPLES AND PRACTICES

▪ *On Running a Business to Win* ▪

B eing a boss is one thing, and managing your career another. But business cannot move forward without certain principles and practices in place.

Right—but which ones? That's the general question that the answers in this chapter grapple with. Grapple, because certain principles, such as candor and differentiation, and certain practices, such as strategy, budgeting, and HR, are controversial, to say the least. Take candor. We haven't visited a country (including the United States) where people haven't challenged its "appropriateness," not to mention its practicality. But every aspect of management, as the following pages show, can be open to debate. And they should be; that's how companies get better.

23

GETTING THE BEST PEOPLE

In your experience, what are the three most critical factors to put in place to turn a company into a "preferred employer" on a sustained basis? And what's a realistic time frame for getting there?

—CHICAGO, ILLINOIS

You ask for three factors—but you really need twice that many "gold stars" to earn the grand prize of being a preferred employer. And it *is* a grand prize, because when you build a company where people really want to work, you've got your hands on one of the most powerful competitive advantages in the game, the ability to hire and field the best team.

But before we give you our six ways to arrive at that fortunate place, a reply to your question about how long the preferred employer process takes.

The answer is easily years, and it can be decades or more. That's just the way it is with corporate reputations—they're built annual report by annual report, career story by career story, crisis by crisis (because every company has one or two of them), and recovery by recovery. It probably took IBM about thirty years to earn its gold-standard reputation in the '70s, less than a decade to lose it when the company stumbled, and then about a decade more to rebuild it to where it is today.

In today's media-saturated world, however, there is a major exception to the generally slow pace of reputation building. Companies can become preferred employers virtually overnight thanks to a "buzz factor," which is as potent as it is fast acting. In a technology-based company, buzz usually comes with an exciting breakthrough or otherwise paradigm-altering new product or service. Google, eBay, and Apple are perfect examples. Buzz, however, can also come from having a glamorous or prestigious brand, like Chanel or Ferrari.

But the buzz factor is as rare as it is precarious. Apple had it with the Mac, lost it when other PC manufacturers leapfrogged them, then recaptured it (plus some) with the iPod. This entirely common story explains why most companies have to become a preferred employer the old-fashioned way, grinding it out over time.

Here's a checklist to assess your company's progress.

First, preferred employers demonstrate a real commitment to continuous learning. No lip service. These companies invest in the development of their people with classes, training programs, and off-site experiences, all sending the message that the organization is eager to facilitate a steady path to personal growth.

Second, preferred employers are meritocracies. Pay and promotions are tightly linked to performance, and rigorous appraisal systems consistently let people know where they stand. As at every company, whom you know and where you went to school might help get you in the door at a meritocracy. But after that, it's all about results. Now, why does all this make a company a preferred employer? Very simply, because people with brains, self-confidence, and competitive spirit are always attracted to such environments.

Third, preferred employers not only allow people to take risks, they celebrate those who do, and don't shoot those who fail trying. As with meritocracies, a culture of risk taking attracts exactly the kind of creative and bold individuals that companies want and need in a global marketplace where innovation is the single best defense against unrelenting cost competition.

Next, preferred employers understand that what is good for society is also good for business. Gender, race, and nationality are never limitations; everyone's ideas matter. Preferred employers are diverse and global in their outlook and environmentally sensitive in their practices. They offer flexibility in work schedules to those who earn it with performance. In a word, preferred companies are enlightened.

Fifth, preferred employers keep their hiring standards tight. They make candidates work hard, requiring an arduous interview process and strict criteria around intelligence and previous experience. Admittedly, this factor is somewhat of a catch-22, as it is difficult to be picky *before* you become an employer of choice! But it's worth the effort, as talent has an uncanny way of attracting, well, talent.

Sixth and finally, preferred companies are profitable and growing. A rising stock price is a real hiring magnet. Beyond that, though, only thriving companies can promise you a future, with career mobility and the potential of increased financial reward. Indeed, one of the most intoxicating things a company can say to a potential employee is, "Join us for the ride of your life."

As we said at the outset, the best thing about being a preferred employer is that it gets you good people—and that launches a virtuous cycle. The best team attracts the best team, and winning often leads to more winning.

That's a ride that you and your employees will never want to get off.

■   ■   ■

24

THE FIGHT AGAINST PHONINESS

Even though my company is in a very competitive industry and we need to move fast and decisively, I've noticed that people rarely say what they mean to each other—particularly in meetings. There's just so much beating around the bush and general phoniness. I'm just a middle manager. What can I do?

—PHOENIX, ARIZONA

What you describe is one of the most common and destructive problems in business, and in society, for that matter—the lack of candor. No matter where we travel, we hear about organizations that are slowed down and gummed up by the very human tendency to soften hard, urgent messages with false kindness or phony optimism. This tendency is particularly prevalent when it comes to communicating about poor performance. Very often, bosses don't come right out and tell underperformers how badly they are doing until, in a burst of frustration, they fire them. That's terribly unfair to the person at the receiving end and often very disruptive to the business itself.

But lack of candor doesn't just pervade performance evaluations. It cripples lots of conversations, many about how and when and where to spend scarce company resources. Yes, these kinds of conversations can be sensitive, politically loaded, or complex, or all of the above. But they'll simply be better if they're candid.

So, what can you do? The only option we know of is having the guts to start using candor yourself, even if you have limited power in the organization. When people use double-talk, push back with questions that cut through the nonsense and probe for reality. Ask, "What are you really trying to tell us?" or say, "What I hear you saying is . . ." and deliver the straight message yourself for confirmation.

Introducing candor to an organization, of course, is not without risk. In fact, it can be a total shock to the system, and being the first one to use it can get you killed, that is, marginalized or thrown out. But should you decide to get candid anyway, go slow and use humor when possible. In the best-case scenario, your candor will eventually be rewarded with candor in return—and sometimes the change is faster than you would imagine. As soon as many people experience candor, they can't understand how they ever did business without it.

■   ■   ■

25

THE LIMITS OF CANDOR—OR NOT

I'm a recent MBA who was just made a manager. I believe in using candor, but I'm afraid to, since most of my direct reports are twice my age.

—HUNTSVILLE, ALABAMA

You may feel squeamish using candor with people who look like your parents, but rest assured that "old people" hate jargon, ambiguity, and double-talk just as much as you do. In fact, having suffered through it at work for decades, they will most likely applaud your efforts to be straight, especially after the shock wears off.

Shock—because without doubt, there will be a rough period of adjustment once you start talking directly and honestly about performance and results. Most people—no matter what their age—just aren't accustomed to it.

Use it anyway. In the end, candor always works, and it always makes work better. Once you dispense with mixed messages and phony performance reviews, a team never fails to become faster, more creative, and more energetic.

And frankly, candor is your job. In fact, once you become a manager, it's your obligation to let everyone who works for you know exactly where they stand. That's how you build the best team—and win.

Your question, by the way, is by no means unusual. We've heard every possible excuse for avoiding candor—it goes against politeness in Japan, for instance, and egalitarianism in Sweden. But by far, the age issue you raise is the most common reason for discomfort.

Let go of it. Some "old folks" might object at first, but the good ones have been waiting longer than you think for straight talk to arrive.

■   ■   ■

26

THE CASE FOR DIFFERENTIATION ...
EVEN IN SWEDEN

You have long advocated a management approach called "differentiation"—promoting the top 20 percent of performers in a company, developing the middle 70, and letting go of the bottom 10. But how can your method be applied in Sweden, where it is not really possible to fire someone who is underachieving?

—GÖTEBORG, SWEDEN

You ask about Sweden, but we've heard this question in dozens of countries, from Germany to Japan to Mexico. We've even heard it in the United States, with its relatively flexible labor laws. There, people ask the variation, "How can I apply differentiation in my company? We never fire anyone—we can't."

It's just not true. Differentiation can be applied anywhere—if it's done right. Yes, there are always people who claim at the outset that the system won't work in *their* culture, but over time, they come to see how differentiation not only helps employees improve their lives, it changes the competitive game. And they come to understand how differentiation isn't at odds with any particular national character or set of labor laws. In fact, quite the contrary.

Look, differentiation raises hackles, as you mention, because of its firing component. The irony is, once the system is in place, it hardly ever ends up with managers terminating anyone. That's because differentiation forces companies to implement regular, candid performance appraisals so that a 20-70-10 curve can be established. When people are told during these appraisals that they are in the bottom 10 percent, they usually move along of their own accord, more often than not finding jobs that fit them better. Almost no one wants to stay where they are at the bottom of the barrel.

Meanwhile, the rest of differentiation does its powerful work. Great performers get rewarded in their souls and pocketbooks, usually increasing their zest to achieve even more, and middling performers get the development and training they need to deliver better results and increase their opportunities for growth. It really is a system where individuals win and the company does too.

That said, it is true that differentiation is an easier sell in some countries than others. You mention legal issues with firing in Sweden, a prospect that immediately sends most managers running for cover. And when we were in Stockholm recently, we heard a lot about the cultural value placed on egalitarianism, not exactly a 20-70-10 kind of concept.

Even in such situations, where differentiation appears to be a challenging cultural fit, managers shouldn't balk. You may have to go more slowly, put more effort into it, and pay more to people with whom you part ways. But the benefits far outweigh these costs. Start by introducing honest appraisals, making sure they are conducted at least twice a year. Let people know where they stand—with no sugar coating or double-talk. Make candor a real organizational value. Talk relentlessly about why the rigorous personnel evaluations at the core of differentiation matter so darned much. After all, they field the best players, and everyone knows that the team with the best players wins.

And who doesn't want that—even in Sweden?

■   ■   ■

27

STRATEGY FOR BIG AND SMALL ALIKE

What do you see as the essentials of strategy for companies employing less than one hundred people? Recommendations from academics and consultants apply almost exclusively to large corporations, drowning us in a sea of advice that just feels irrelevant for small organizations with constrained resources.

—PITTSBURG, KANSAS

We might have bad news for you. Strategy is strategy, whether the company is large or small. It's that killer idea—a "big aha" as we call it—that gives you a sustainable competitive advantage. Put another way, strategy is just a winning value proposition, that is, a product or service that customers simply want more than the other options out there. Beyond that, strategy is all in its execution—and on that front, small companies actually have something of an advantage.

Now, we don't blame you for feeling as if most of the

advice on strategy that you hear today applies mainly to big companies. It's all so complex, as if strategy is some kind of high-brain scientific methodology. In fact, with the arduous, intellectualized number crunching and data analysis being promoted, well . . . you'd *have* to be a large company to have the people, time, and money to attempt it.

Don't bother. The more you grind down into details and different scenarios, the more you get tied up in knots. Look, once you have your big aha, strategy is just a general direction. It's an approximate course of action that you revisit and redefine according to shifting market conditions. It's got to feel fluid—it's got to be alive!

Small companies—and large ones—can actually come up with their strategy just by probing five key questions. What does the competitive playing field look like? What have our competitors been up to lately? What have we done lately? What future events or possible changes keep us up at night with worry? And given all that, what's our winning move?

This relatively fast, theory-free process obviously doesn't require an academic textbook or consultants to complete. In fact, it requires only a team of informed, engaged employees who can dream big and debate intensely—and ultimately emerge with a dynamic game plan.

Then it's time to implement, and that's when small companies really have it made. When there are only one hundred employees, or even a thousand, it is just so much easier to communicate strategy and get people excited about it with a shared, contagious intensity and spirit of can-do. And once the strategy is launched, small companies, like little powerboats, are able to adjust direction more quickly than corporate ocean liners. They can also hire faster, make decisions with fewer bureaucratic hurdles, and generally see their mistakes (and fix them) sooner than hulking rivals.

With that said, small isn't totally beautiful when it comes to strategy. Here's the rub: with constrained resources, you have to be right more often. Big companies can take a lot of swings; they can afford to invest in one or two or three big ahas that don't work out. By contrast, one big strategy mistake can put a small company out of business.

The imperative for small companies, then, is to hold their value proposition to a higher standard. They really have to make sure they've got something singular—a new idea with a patent, a breakthrough technology, an extremely low-cost process, or a unique service offering. Whatever—it just has to have the power to attract customers and make them stick.

And when they do, small companies can celebrate a strategy that's winning, knowing they did it without all the charts, graphs, reports, studies, and big fat stacks of PowerPoint slides that no one really needs, not even the big guys.

■   ■   ■

28

THE CONSULTANT CONUNDRUM

Are consultants good or bad? Under what circumstances would you bring them in, and what does bringing them in say about the skills of your own people?

—ALBANY, NEW YORK

Your question is sort of like asking, "Are doctors good or bad?" The answer is, some are good and some are bad—but either way, you want to spend as little time with them as you can.

Look, the problem with consultants is they're fundamentally (if surreptitiously) at loggerheads with the managers they want to work for. Consultants want to come into a company, solve its mess, and then hang around finding and solving other messes—*forever.* Managers want consultants to come in, solve their specific problem fast, and get out, also forever. The tension between these conflicting goals is what makes the use of consultants intractably problematic.

There are, of course, situations when consultants are useful. Sometimes a company needs fresh eyes to assess an old strategy or a new product. Sometimes a company simply does not have the in-house skills needed to make an informed decision. Private equity firms today, for example, use consultants very effectively to quickly evaluate the markets and industries of potential acquisitions.

But the byword with consultants is "Be careful." Before you know it, they could be doing the ongoing work of your business. After all, that's what they want, even if you don't.

■　■　■

29

THE DANGER OF DOING NOTHING

Five years ago, we started a company in the then red-hot fiber communication industry. We've fought hard to stay viable, but now it's obvious that the "growth space" for our company is much more limited than we'd hoped for. Should we give up and start again in a new area or stay in the survival game?

—SUNNYVALE, CALIFORNIA

Since you're from Silicon Valley, it seems to us that you probably know the answer to your question: the survival game stinks, perhaps no place more than the technology sector. In fact, sticking it out in a low-growth technology business is a fast road to commodity hell, where you will be forced to endure a painful eternity of low-cost slugfests with offshore manufacturers. What a way *not* to go.

Clearly, then, you would be better off finding a new area where you and your team can grow and flourish.

It appears your company has a business model where survival, at least for the foreseeable future, is an option. That's good news. It means your immediate challenge will be harvesting the living daylights out of what you have to keep the cash flow coming. Meanwhile, you can figure out the new game, allocating the resources to acquire a business or start one from scratch.

Now, none of this may seem particularly easy or particularly pleasant—exiting a business rarely is—but you can take solace in knowing that your situation is entirely common. The environment starts to change under your feet, and suddenly your business doesn't make that much sense anymore. This happens every day, all over the world, not just in entrepreneurial start-ups. In fact, it's particularly common at older, established companies, where new competitive dynamics emerge seemingly out of nowhere to upend the status quo. Unfortunately, all too often in these big companies, certain businesses have become such shrines that managers do not react with the kind of clear-eyed realism that your letter suggests.

Look, change requires leaders to overcome all sorts of completely human dynamics, like inertia, fondness for tradition, and hopefulness that things will get better. But strategic moments require a kind of courage, or at least a lack of sentimentality, which is rare. It is in these moments that the best leaders find a mirror and ask the defining question that the late, great Peter Drucker posed nearly fifty years ago: "If you weren't already in your business, would you enter it today?" If the answer was no, Drucker said, you needed to face into a second tough question: "What are you going to do about it?" Every leader today should heed his advice and, if need be, follow it through to its conclusion, whether it is to fix, sell, or close the business.

Congratulations for having done that already. Your decision may be tough in the short run, but it will ultimately release your people from a losing work environment and give them a chance to find a future filled with opportunities, perhaps even with your new venture.

■   ■   ■

30

HOW HEALTHY IS YOUR COMPANY?

If you had to pick, which three measurements would
you say give the best sense of a company's health?

—ORLANDO, FLORIDA

Every type of business, not to mention every type
of manager, has a different set of vital statistics
that really matter. For manufacturing people, it could
be inventory turns, on-time delivery, and unit cost. For
marketing people, it could be new account closings, market share, and sales growth. For call center managers, it
could be time to answer, the number of dropped calls,
and employee retention.

But if you're running a business, whether it's a corner
store or a multiproduct multinational, we'd say there are
three key indicators that really work: employee engagement, customer satisfaction, and cash flow.

These measurements won't tell you everything you
need to know, but close to it. They get right to the guts

of a company's overall performance, now and in the future.

Employee engagement first. It goes without saying that no company, small or large, can win over time without energized employees who believe in the mission and understand how to achieve it. That's why you need to test for employee engagement at least once a year in anonymous surveys where people feel completely safe to speak their minds.

But watch out. Do not fall into the common trap of letting these surveys devolve into the little stuff, with questions about the quality of food in the company cafeteria or the availability of parking spaces in the company lot. The best, most meaningful employee engagement surveys are a world apart from that. They probe how employees feel about the strategic direction of the company and the quality of their career opportunities. They ask, "Do you believe the company has a set of goals that people fully grasp, accept, and support?" and "Do you feel the company cares about you and that you have been given the opportunity to grow?" and "Do you feel that your everyday work is connected to what company leaders say in their speeches and in the annual report?"

Basically, the best employee engagement surveys are getting at one question: "Are we all on the same team here?"

Of course, growth is the key to long-term viability, which is why customer satisfaction is the second vital sign for general managers. Again, this measurement can be obtained by surveys, but those are rarely enough to give you the gritty data you need for a real read of the situation. No, you need to make visits. And don't just go chat with your "good" customers. Go to see the most difficult, the ones whose orders are inconsistent or dropping. Go to see the ones your salespeople don't like to see themselves.

Make these visits about learning. Find a dozen ways to ask, "What can we do better?" And don't leave without finding out if each customer would recommend your products or services. That's the acid test of customer satisfaction.

Finally, there's cash flow, which is valuable because it just does not lie. All your other P & L numbers, like net income, have some art to them. They've been massaged through the accounting process, which is filled with assumptions. But free cash flow tells you the true condition of the business. It gives you a sense of your maneuverability—whether you can return cash to shareholders, pay down debt, or borrow more to grow faster, or any combination of these options. Cash flow, basically, helps you understand and control your destiny.

Without doubt, there are plenty of measurements

that give you a pulse of your business. But if you have employee engagement, customer satisfaction, and cash flow right, you can be sure your company is healthy— and well on the way to winning.

■   ■   ■

31

THE REAL JOB OF HR

If HR is the most powerful part of an organization, as you always say, why is its impact only felt in a negative way?

—LOUISVILLE, KENTUCKY

Because at too many companies, unfortunately, HR gets it wrong—either operating as a cloak-and-dagger society or a health-and-happiness sideshow. Those are extremes, of course, but if there is anything we have learned over the past five years of traveling, it is that HR rarely functions as HR should.

That's an outrage, made only more so by the fact that most leaders aren't scrambling to fix it.

Point blank: HR should be every single company's killer app. What could possibly be more important than who gets hired, developed, promoted, or moved out the door? After all, business is a game, and as with all games, the team that puts the best people on the field and gets them playing together wins. It's that simple.

You would never know that, though, to look at the companies today where the CFO reigns supreme and HR is relegated to the background. It just doesn't make sense. If you owned the Red Sox, for instance, would you hang around with the team accountant or the director of player personnel? Sure, the accountant can tell you the financials. But the director of player personnel knows what it takes to win: how good each player is and where to find strong recruits to fill talent gaps.

That's what HR should be all about.

And as you point out, it's usually not.

That was never as painfully clear to us as it was several years ago when we spoke to five thousand HR professionals in Mexico City. At one point, we asked the audience, "How many of you work at companies where the CEO gives HR a seat at the table equal to that of the CFO?" After an awkward silence, fewer than fifty people raised their hands. Awful!

Since then, we've tried to understand why HR has become so marginalized, and as noted above, there are at least two poles of bad behavior. The cloak-and-dagger stuff occurs when HR managers become stealthy little kingmakers, making and breaking careers, sometimes not even at the CEO's behest. These HR departments can indeed be powerful but often in a detrimental way, prompting the best people to leave just to get away from the palace intrigue of it all. Just as often, though, you get the other extreme: HR departments that plan picnics, put out the plant newsletter, and generally drive everyone crazy by enforcing rules and regulations that appear to have no purpose other than to increase bureaucracy. They derive the little power they have by being the "You can't do that" police.

So, how do leaders fix this mess?

It all starts with the people they appoint to run HR— not kingmakers or cops but big leaguers, people with real stature and credibility. In fact, they need to fill HR with a special kind of hybrid: people who are one part pastor, hearing all sins and complaints without recrimination, and one part parent, loving and nurturing but giving it to you straight when you're off track. Pastor-parent types can rise through HR, but more often than not, they have run something during their careers, such as a factory or a function. They *get* the business—its inner workings, its history and tensions, the hidden hierarchies in people's minds. They are known to be relentlessly candid, even when the message is hard, and hold confidences tight. Indeed, with their insight and integrity, pastor-parents earn the trust of the organization.

But pastor-parents don't just sit around making people feel warm and fuzzy. They make the company better, first and foremost by overseeing a rigorous appraisal and evaluation system that lets every person in the organization know where he or she stands, and monitoring that system with the same intensity of Sarbanes-Oxley compliance.

Leaders should also make sure that HR fulfills two other roles. It should create effective mechanisms, such as money, recognition, and training, to motivate and retain people. And it should spur organizations to face into their most charged relationships, such as those with unions, individuals who are no longer delivering results, or stars who are becoming problematic by, for instance, swelling instead of growing.

Now, given your negative experience with HR—and you are hardly alone—this kind of high-impact HR activity probably sounds like a pipe dream. But given the fact that most CEOs loudly proclaim that people are their "biggest asset," it shouldn't be.

It can't be. Leaders need to put their money where their mouth is and get HR do its real job: elevating people management to the same level of professionalism and integrity as financial management.

Since people are the whole game, what could be more important?

■   ■   ■

32

STAFF FUNCTIONARIES...
AND OTHER FILTERS

I work for a manufacturing company where the IT department reports to the head of finance. He never has time to evaluate IT projects, so it ends up that IT, which has no representation at the board level, gets attention only when there is a burning issue. This is a problem, isn't it?

—HARARE, ZIMBABWE

It sure is. In fact, that sound you hear is the collective groan of hordes of people, just like you, who have watched this dysfunctional dynamic play out in their own organizations. And we're not just talking about IT getting buried where it shouldn't and neglected until a crisis strikes—although that's bad enough. We're talking about the bigger and more onerous problem your letter suggests—the Rasputin-like dominance of the chief financial officer in too many companies.

OK, maybe invoking Rasputin is a bit extreme. But it's not going too far to say that the CFO can, and very often does, wield too much influence. And if not the CFO, it's the so-called chief administrative officer who gets this type of excessive power, overseeing finance itself, HR, and any number of other staff departments. Now, sometimes the chief administrative officer is the former CFO. Sometimes he or she is the former general counsel. Regardless, this extra management layer spawns bureaucracy at its worst. The person holding the CFO or chief administrative officer title inevitably becomes the company's go-to guy—the bodyguard through whom every question and decision must pass before finally making it to the CEO—or not. The job becomes a catchall bin for projects, people, or whole departments that the "overburdened" CEO, with just too many direct reports, is said to be too busy to deal with.

It's just wrong.

So, why does it happen?

With IT, the explanation is easy: it's a historical hangover. Initially, IT was mainly seen as good for lowering the costs and increasing the efficiency of payroll operations. In those days, decades ago, there was some logic to having IT report to the CFO. Most good companies, however, took IT out of finance when its broad strategic utility became obvious. But some, apparently including your company, have not.

As for HR reporting to a chief administrative officer, there actually can be no good explanation! With its critical role in hiring, appraising, and developing people, HR is so central to the success of a company, it's practically criminal if it doesn't report directly to the CEO. When it doesn't, you can only assume it's because the CEO doesn't get the people thing, or someone else is actually running the place, or both.

Which brings us to the consequences of this whole dynamic. The first is that frontline IT and HR managers, who usually have among the most relevant ideas and information in the company, do not get heard high enough up in a timely way. Any insights they might have get filtered before making it to the CEO or the board, sometimes by the cost-sensitive CFO, of all people!

Second, companies where the CFO or chief administrative officer reigns supreme have a much harder time attracting good people to top HR and IT jobs. The best and brightest in these fields will always choose to work where they have a seat at the table *equal* to the CFO. Why shouldn't they? The best companies recognize their value and reward them with pay and prestige.

So, to your question then—absolutely, IT shouldn't be reporting to the CFO.

Nor, for that matter, should any key function report to a bureaucratic layer. Your painfully common problem is case in point.

■   ■   ■

33

STOPPING JOB CUTS
BEFORE THEY HAPPEN

When a company is going through a hard time, it usually makes job cuts. Isn't that hypocritical, since most companies claim people are their "most valuable asset" and spend a lot of money on training as well?

—CURITIBA, BRAZIL

Sometimes companies have no choice but layoffs. They miss a technology cycle or the economy in general is tanking. But the awful truth is that too many companies use tough times to do something they should be doing all along—cleaning house. That negligence—especially while numbly chanting the "people are our most valuable asset" mantra—certainly makes sudden layoffs hypocritical, as you suggest.

But more than that, it makes them unfair and cruel.

Look, it's not always easy to be a manager, but once you agree to be one, you have a responsibility to your employees, and that is to always let them know where they stand. No company should be without a rigorous appraisal system, and no manager should be too weak-kneed to implement it. Rewards should be closely linked to an employee's evaluation, with the most money and praise going to the best, and nothing at all going to the worst.

This kind of system has a swift and amazing effect on underperformers. You rarely have to fire them. They usually leave on their own. And in fact, many of them go on to find work that better fits their skills, at places where they can finally be appreciated. It's a perfect ending for them, the company they've left, and the one they've joined.

The problem is that many managers claim they are too "kind" or too "nice" to tell people exactly where they stand—in particular, the real losers.

That's why so many companies run into the situation you describe. The pattern usually goes like this. Faced with poor results, the top team decides costs must be reduced fast. Managers throughout the company see layoffs as the most immediate course of action, so the manager of, say, division Q, decides to fire two people. Now, all along, this terribly nice person has been telling his employees how great they are, rewarding them about equally at bonus time and even sending many of them off for training. But when the boom falls, he knows *exactly* who should go: Joe and Mary, who haven't carried their weight for years.

He calls each of them in for a meeting to give the news.

"Why me?" both ask.

"Well, because you weren't very good" is the mumbled answer.

"But I've been told I was doing just fine for thirty years! What's going on?"

Good question.

If this manager had been doing his personnel job the right way all along, being fired wouldn't have come as such a shock to poor Joe and Mary. Knowing their status, they would have left the company long before. Instead, they find themselves forced to look for new work, often during the very recession that made their layoffs necessary.

So much for "kind" management.

Now, we're not saying that companies can always avoid the shock and pain of layoffs by consistently using a system of appraisals and housecleaning. There will always be unfortunate events outside an organization's control that require fast cost-cutting, and nothing does that like job cuts.

But a rigorous evaluation system combined with clear

communication about how the company is faring go a long way toward preventing the kind of widespread cynicism about layoffs that you exemplify—and rightly so.

■   ■   ▨

34

NO MORE B.S. BUDGETING

The longer I work, the more I get the feeling that even the best people waste their time "delivering the budget." I guess that has to happen, but the whole budgeting process just seems so senseless. Your opinion?

—PRAGUE, CZECH REPUBLIC

Senseless? Not really—counterproductive is more like it.

Look, some form of financial planning is obviously necessary; companies have to keep track of the numbers. But your thinking is on the right track. The budgeting process—as it currently stands at most companies—does exactly what you'd never want. It hides growth opportunities. It promotes bad behaviors, in particular when market conditions change midstream and people *still* try to "make the number." And it has an uncanny way of sucking the energy and fun out of an organization.

Why? Because most budgeting is, simply put, disconnected from reality. It's a process that draws its authority from the mere fact that it's institutionalized, as in: "Well, that's just the way it's always been done."

It just doesn't have to be!

But before we go there—that is, a better way to budget—think about what's wrong with the standard approach.

The process usually begins in the early fall. That's when the people in the field start the long slog of constructing the next year's bottom-up, highly detailed financial plans to make their case to the company bigwigs in a few weeks' time. The goal of the people in the field, of course, is unstated, but it's laserlike. They want to come up with targets that they absolutely, positively think they can hit; after all, that's how they're rewarded. So, they construct plans with layer upon layer of conservatism.

Meanwhile, back at headquarters, executives are also preparing for the budget review, but with the exact opposite agenda. They're rewarded for big increases in sales and earnings, so they want targets that push the limits.

You know what happens next. The two sides meet in a windowless room for a daylong wrestling match. The field will make the case that competition is brutal and the economy is tough, and, therefore, earnings can increase, say, just 6 percent. Headquarters will look surprised and perhaps a bit irate; their view of the world calls for the team to deliver 14 percent.

Fast-forward to late in the day. Despite the requisite groaning and grumbling along the way, the budget number will be settled right down the middle—10 percent. And soon after, the meeting will end with pleasantries and handshakes. It will only be later, when both sides are alone, that they will crow among themselves about how they managed to get the other guys to *exactly* the targets they wanted.

What's wrong with this picture? First, what you see: an orchestrated compromise. But more important, what you don't: a rich, expansive conversation about growth opportunities, especially the high-risk ones.

That conversation is usually missing because of the wrongheaded reward system we mentioned above. People in the field are literally paid to hit their targets. They get a stick in the eye (or worse) for missing them. So, why in the world would they ever dream big?

They won't—unless a new reward system is put in place. One in which bonuses are based *not* on an internally negotiated number but on real-world measures: how the business performed compared to the previous year and how it did compared to the competition.

With those kinds of metrics, watch out. Suddenly,

budgeting can change from a mind-numbing ritual to a wide-ranging, anything-goes dialogue between the field and headquarters about gutsy, what-if market opportunities. And from those conversations will spring growth scenarios that cannot really be called budgets at all. They're *operating plans*, filled with mutually agreed-upon strategies and tactics to expand sales and earnings, not all of them sure bets.

Of course, operating plans are not all wishing and fluff, lacking any financial framework. They should always contain an upside number—the best-case scenario—and a number below which the business is not expected to go. The main point is, though, that this range will be the result of a dialogue about market realities.

And because they're part of a dialogue, operating plans can be flexible, changing during the year with market conditions if need be.

In fact, the only rigid thing about this form of budgeting is the core value it requires of an organization— and that is trust. People in the field have to believe they won't be punished for not reaching their stretch targets, and executives have to honor that confidence. Executives, meanwhile, have to believe that people in the field are giving their all to achieve those big goals, and people in the field have to uphold that good faith with their efforts.

With that "contract" in place, the budget dynamic takes on a whole new life.

So, don't give up on budgeting at your company yet. You're right to be frustrated by it now, but given how much is to be gained, maybe it's time to start a conversation about changing the process. Are you ready?

■   ■   ■

35

NOT INVENTED WHERE?

Our automotive parts company employs about two thousand people and has a long history of technical and manufacturing expertise, but very little in the way of marketing. Here's my problem: we currently have a product that is technically perfect, but customers aren't buying it. (They prefer another, more advanced solution, made by a competitor.) Obviously, to stay competitive, we need to lower the price, but I just don't see how. Our costs are so well managed that outsourcing, even from China, India, or Eastern Europe, seems pointless. Moreover, we have the most suitable manufacturing technology available, and our machinery depreciations are very low at the moment. What's your advice?

—PRAGUE, CZECH REPUBLIC

For someone at a company of only two thousand people, you sure sound as if you have one of the most common symptoms of big company-itis: the not invented here syndrome, or NIH.

You know NIH. It's when managers become very comfortable with the notion that their company is performing at its peak—so comfortable, in fact, that they create an atmosphere where there is little interest in using ideas from outside sources to improve how things are done. NIH managers believe the company has everything figured out. After all, it's been around for a while and had its share of successes. "This is the way we do it here," they like to say. And should someone suggest a new practice, they typically come back with the refrain, "We've tried that before."

Now, big company-itis in general is awful. Along with NIH's complacency, its other symptoms include inertia, bureaucracy, and risk aversion. But NIH trumps them all. It wrecks organizations, draining competitiveness right from the veins.

So, let's talk about cures.

In fact, let's look at your situation. You indicate that you have costs so under control that they can go no lower, even with outsourcing. You also seem to believe you have the best technology available, further obviating the need to seek alternatives outside the company. Overall, you seem genuinely stymied by your problem.

But perhaps you see no way out because you're too inwardly focused. To us, your problem seems pretty straightforward. A competitor appears to have built a better, cheaper "mousetrap" than you and gotten it to market faster. The solution feels straightforward too: why not let go of the notion that you've tried everything and try *more* of everything?

Innovation, basically, is what we're talking about. Your company has to become fixated on finding a new process, product, or service that creates a value proposition the market desperately wants to buy. Maybe a new practice is what you need—a different way of purchasing, or a new way of communicating with customers. Maybe a new technology will move you forward—something you can develop or get from another company through a license, merger, or acquisition. With an open mind you'll find the world of improvement possibilities is huge. In fact, keep pushing on the outsourcing front. Despite your excellent machines and low depreciation, there has to be a company in a country out there that can make your product's components or the finished product itself for less.

Your greatest advantage at this time, ironically, may be your size. Your company is too small to have big company-itis! With two thousand people you should be able to move quickly to develop and push a new technology through testing, or buy another company with a great add-on service, or change management to bring in fresh faces who can break the technical paradigm. The biggest thing standing in the way is your attitude—an insular big-company condition you can't afford to have.

■   ■   ■

36

MAKING SENSE OF MATRIXES

Having worked in both large and small organizations, I am at a loss to see the overall benefits of matrix organizational structures. Is this a problem inherent with the matrix structure or just poor matrix management?

—COLORADO SPRINGS, COLORADO

It's so easy to hate matrixes, isn't it? If there is one thing practically everyone in business can agree on, it's that they sound great in theory but are hell to put into practice.

Count us in. We sure prefer pure P & L businesses. They're built on clear reporting relationships, making each individual accountable for his or her results. They make strategic focus and resource allocation easier. They're better training grounds for developing general managers. And they're definitely better when it comes to creating new businesses out of the old; in P & L struc-tures, start-up champions just have an easier time get-ting heard.

Meanwhile, matrixes, for all their good intentions, can be exercises in frustration. Their biggest problem: sucking the clarity right out of organizations. Any time you have someone reporting to two bosses, chances are accountability will get muddled. Matrixes are filled with dotted-line relationships. The result can be all sorts of mischief, from power plays to miscommunications. At the same time, matrixes often put well-meaning people at total cross-purposes. One classic matrix scenario in-volves a manufacturing manager trying to make his overall inventory budget at the expense of a product manager with a hot new widget who is crying for avail-ability. No wonder matrixes tend to enervate the people who work in them—ambiguity and loggerheads have a way of doing that.

But if matrixes were all bad, they'd be as extinct as dinosaurs by now, and they're not.

Matrixes have two main advantages. The first is that they create a well of superior expertise that many product lines can draw on. Take, for example, a jet en-gine company with several different engine types. In a P & L situation, each engine type would have its own metallurgist. But none of these individuals would likely be of the caliber of specialists working in a matrix organization. Why? Because functional organizations—with their pay, visibility, and prestige—are just better able to attract high-level talent.

The second advantage of a matrix is financial. With their larger orders, the heads of manufacturing and marketing in a matrix are far better equipped to drive a hard bargain with suppliers and distributors than the heads of individual P & L businesses. They just have more negotiating power.

So, while working in a matrix can sometimes be maddening, the structure's benefits cannot be denied. From your question, it's difficult to tell exactly why the experience has been so negative for you. Perhaps, as you imply, it has something to do with management. That wouldn't surprise us; matrixes are harder to run than pure P & L businesses. They require a higher comfort level with ambiguity. Further, they require a higher level of trust. That is, the people in the product lines have to believe to their toes that the people in the functions are working for the business's overall goal, not just to make their own numbers.

Bottom line: matrixes may never be as great in practice as they are in theory, and they will never be as easy to work in as a pure P & L, but don't give up on them altogether.

When leaders build trust and push hard to ensure as much clarity as possible, matrixes do work.

■   ■   ■

37

THE USES AND ABUSES OF GUT INSTINCT

What would you do if you found out that your employees had a tendency to rely more on gut instinct than on facts and rational thinking? Mine do, making me wonder how I can possibly explain their decisions to company executives.

—JAKARTA, INDONESIA

You really have two choices. Either tell your bosses, "Charlie made that terrific decision based on his tried-and-true gut instinct," or, if Charlie's gut is fifty-fifty at best, ask him to stop making decisions that way.

Look, as a general rule, gut instinct is nothing to be ashamed of. Quite the opposite. It's really just pattern recognition, isn't it? You've seen something so many times over your life or career, you just get what's going on this time. Gut instinct, in other words, is a deep, perhaps even subconscious, familiarity—the kind of knowing that tells you anything from, "Go for it *now*," to "No way—*not ever.*" Although we would wager the most common gut call falls in between the two—the "uh-oh" response, in which your stomach informs you that something is not right and you should figure out what it is.

The trick with gut, of course, is to know when to trust it. That's an easy call when you discover, over time, that your gut is usually right. But such confidence can take years of trial and error.

Until that point, we suggest this rule of thumb: gut calls are usually pretty helpful when it comes to looking at deals and less so when it comes to picking people.

No, we're not mixing them up. Even though deals come to you with all sorts of data analysis and detailed quantitative predictions, and people decisions seem so much more qualitative, the numbers in deal books are really just projections. Sometimes those projections are reasonable, but in other cases, they're little more than wishful thinking. When have you ever been presented with a deal with a projected discounted rate of return less than 20 percent? You haven't! Again, sometimes that's because a deal is great. But other times that's because the people proposing the deal have adjusted the investment's residual value to make the returns reflect their hopes and prayers.

So, when it comes to looking at deals, consider the numbers—of course. But make sure your gut plays a big

role in the final call as well. Say you've been asked to invest in a new office building, but visiting the city, you see
cranes in every direction. The deal's numbers are perfect, you're told; you simply *can't* lose. But your gut tells
you otherwise—that overcapacity is about a year away
and the "perfect" investment is about to be worth sixty
cents on the dollar. You've got few facts, but you have
the uh-oh response.

More often than not, that means you should kill the
deal, even if it infuriates the so-called rational thinkers
on the case. Odds are, they'll give you credit for pro-
phetic thinking down the road (although probably with
less public gusto than you'd like).

By contrast, relying on your gut during hiring isn't
always a great idea. The reason: our gut often makes us
fall in love with a candidate too quickly. We see a perfect
résumé with prestigious schools and great experience.
We see a likable individual who says all the right things
in the interview. And even though we don't admit it, too
often we also see a person who can quickly make a problem go away, namely, a big, open, gaping position. So,
with our gut hurrying us along, we rush to seal the deal.

We see this dynamic in action all the time when people call us for references. They start off by firmly stating
that they only want an unvarnished view of the candidate in question, but as we start to give it to them, we

can feel them begin to wither. Their voices tighten; it's almost as if they're saying, "Oh, please don't tell me that! All I really wanted from you was a stamp of approval!" They can't get off the phone fast enough.

So, when it comes to hiring decisions, you may want to ask your people to muster up the discipline to doubt and double-check their gut, and you should too. That means dig for extra data about every candidate. Go beyond the résumé. And yes, make reference calls—and make sure to force yourself to listen, especially to mixed messages and unpleasant insights.

Overall, however, gut calls do play a real role in business—and a good one. Don't worry too much about explaining that to your bosses and shareholders. They use theirs too.

■   ■   ■

38

WHAT BECOMES A SALESPERSON MOST

Revenue growth is at the top of my to-do list. What should I look for in hiring great sales professionals?

—WESTFIELD, NEW JERSEY

Good news. You're halfway there because you realize that great salespeople are different from you, us, and most everyone. In fact, they're a breed apart.

Which is not to say that salespeople shouldn't have the qualities you look for in every hire—integrity, intelligence, positive energy, decisiveness, and the ability to execute. It's just that they need other qualities as well—four to be exact.

The first is enormous empathy. Great salespeople *feel* for their customers. They understand their needs and pressures; they *get* the challenges of their business. They see every deal through the customer's eyes. Yes, they represent the company, and yes, they want to make it profitable. But they are geniuses at balancing the interests of the company and the interests of the customer so that, even at the end of difficult negotiations, both sides describe the process as more than fair.

Not surprisingly, then, the second quality of great salespeople is trustworthiness. Their word is good; their handshake means something. They see every sale as part of a long-term relationship, and customers usually respond in kind.

Third, great salespeople have a powerful mixture of drive, courage, and self-confidence. Cold calls are brutal. No one likes making them. But the best salespeople want to grow the business so badly that they dive into them relentlessly, day after day, and they have the inner strength not to take inevitable rejections personally. They just take a deep breath and move on.

Finally, the best salespeople hate the "postman" model of doing business. No offense to letter carriers! It's their job to deliver mail along a set route every day. And great salespeople certainly do a version of that too, selling current products to current customers. But they can't help themselves—they also love to go off-road in search of product and customer opportunities. The best salespeople, for instance, think it's part of their job to regularly bring ideas home from the outer reaches, saying things like, "You know, if we could make XYZ, we could capture a whole new market out there."

In that way, then, the best salespeople *are* just like you. Revenue growth is at the top of *their* to-do list.

Unlike you, or any boss for that matter, concerned with every variety of other organizational matters, revenue growth is also at the middle and bottom.

And that's what makes great salespeople so special— and so valuable.

■   ■   ■

39

THE SLIPPERY SLOPE OF OPEN BOOKS

I run a small shop—just five employees. Lately, I've been thinking about sharing my financials with the team, hoping they'll come to see why we need to be efficient every hour of every day and minimize absenteeism. I'm also hoping that "exposing" our numbers could build teamwork and foster innovation. What's your advice?

—CHERRY HILL, NEW JERSEY

Surely you know the old saying "No good deed goes unpunished." Well, you might be using it yourself very soon.

Not to disparage transparency! In general, the more information you share with employees about costs and other competitive challenges, the better. It's as you suggest—when people know what they're up against, they can feel a greater sense of ownership and urgency, often sparking homegrown improvements in processes and productivity. And the sense that "we're all in this together" can certainly jump-start teamwork and innovation.

But . . .

There are real perils involved with opening the books, the main one being that it's very hard to open them just a little bit. Once you start "exposing" costs to have them make sense, you need to expose revenues and profits as well.

So, are you sure you're comfortable with the team knowing how much the business makes? They will naturally compare that number to what they make, and eventually they will be able to extrapolate how much of the pie you have—and they don't.

That gap may very well be something you're willing or even proud to explain. If so, then there's probably no downside to sharing financial details with your team. But remember that every employee, no matter what size the company, has a personal pay scale in his head that estimates what he and every one of his coworkers is worth based on their output and performance. If you get the sense that your information spree will upend those notions, then leave this particular deed undone for now, and try to find other, perhaps less perilous ways to get your team to care about work the way you do.

■   ■   ■

40

PREVENTING A
CORPORATE KATRINA

The handling of Hurricane Katrina in New Orleans was such a disaster. What organizational lessons can be learned from what went wrong?

—NEWARK, DELAWARE

Hurricane Katrina was, sadly, the perfect storm, in that several terrible things went wrong all at once. Nature delivered a devastating blow, and several government agencies that should have helped (and could have) did very little. It's unfortunate, but for years to come, people will likely be sorting out all the "owners" of the Katrina crisis.

Even now, however, it is clear that one of those owners will be FEMA, the Federal Emergency Management Agency, which technically had über-responsibility for the governmental response to Hurricane Katrina. As everyone now knows, FEMA basically fell apart during the storm in a frenzy of bureaucratic hand-wringing and buck-passing.

It's easy to get frustrated, or worse, by FEMA's performance during Hurricane Katrina. But at the same time, FEMA offers us a perfect example of a completely common organizational dynamic: what happens when one part of an organization is an orphan, neglected and pushed out of sight. In business, the divisions, teams, or departments that are orphans usually get sold or closed. In New Orleans, the consequences of orphanhood were much more tragic.

FEMA was an organizational orphan if ever there was one. For decades, it was a relatively small, independent federal entity with a clear mission to protect life and property during natural disasters. In that capacity, FEMA performed quite well. In 2003, however, FEMA was tucked into the Department of Homeland Security, a sprawling federal entity with a clear mission to protect Americans from *un*natural disasters, i.e., terrorist attacks.

Talk about losing your relevance! The bosses at Homeland Security were understandably worried about train bombings like those in Madrid and subway bombings as in London, not to mention planes plowing into buildings and chemical warfare. The real life-and-death stuff. FEMA was worried about wind and rain, earthquakes and tornados. It was miles away from mission critical. Orphans always are.

And so when orphans shout for help, the mission critical leadership usually doesn't jump. They don't even hear the calls. We don't know for sure, but in the case of Katrina, that appears to be what happened.

The lesson for organizations is to never let orphans develop or reorient them if they do. If a team, department, or entire division seems peripheral to the large organization's mission, put it someplace in the company where it is closer to the core strategy or sell it. Because if you let orphans hang around, you can be certain that eventually no good will come of it. Think of what happened to Frigidaire, the appliance-manufacturing unit of General Motors, which was a pioneer in the industry and held on to a strong market leadership position for decades. Household appliances were hardly mission critical for GM—as the case would be at any car company—and Frigidaire never got the people and resources it needed from headquarters. By the time it was sold off in 1979 to White Consolidated Industries, it had lost much of its market share and was in a significantly weakened competitive position.

There were plenty of orphans at GE; most big companies have them. While loads of money and attention were showered on high-powered engines, the small-engine business was relegated to a state of not-so-benign neglect. It would have completely missed the burgeoning market for commuter jet engines had it not been for one of its senior managers, who demanded to be taken seriously. He proved how and why small engines serving the new commuter jet business could be mission critical to GE, and eventually the division got the resources it deserved and needed in order to grow.

That was a story with a happy ending. The facts are that the stories of many orphans over the years at GE had plots that sound a lot more like Frigidaire.

A major lesson, then, of Hurricane Katrina is one that business has to relearn all the time. Letting one part of an organization remain an orphan, muddling though life in a place far away from mission critical, can have dire consequences.

It's not a matter of if. It's a matter of when.

■   ■   ■

41

WHAT'S HOLDING WOMEN BACK

There still aren't very many women CEOs, and in some countries, not even that many women who are executives. What's the real reason women can't seem to get ahead in the corporate world?

— NEW BERN, NORTH CAROLINA

The easy answer to your question is that the corporate world is fundamentally sexist. The men in charge don't want women to succeed, and they conspire to make it so by not promoting women or underpaying them or both. This is basically the "men are Neanderthals" explanation for the underrepresentation of women in business, and sadly, in some countries and companies, it's the status quo. Mainly due to cultural traditions or ingrained biases, there are men who simply think women don't belong in corporate settings, and they band together to create work environments where women can't move up, even if they try like crazy. This

banding together, by the way, is usually subtle and surreptitious. Sometimes men themselves don't even realize they are doing it. Regardless, they are, and women
pay the price.

There is a second, less easy answer to your question,
and we say less easy because every time we mention it in
speeches, it provokes a real gasp of discomfort from the
audience. That answer is "biology." There are very few
women CEOs and a disproportionately small number of
women senior executives because women have babies.
And despite what some earnest but misguided social
pundits might tell you, that matters. Because when professional women decide to have children, they often decide to cut back their hours at work or travel less. Some
women change jobs entirely, to staff positions with more
flexibility but much lower visibility. Still more women
actually leave the workforce entirely. In fact, a 2002
survey conducted by Harvard Business School of its
alumnae from the classes of 1981, 1986, and 1991 showed
that 62 percent had left the professional world. That's
right—out of all the women who graduated in those
classes, many of them immediately going on to jobs in
consulting, finance, and line management, only 38 percent were still working full-time some ten, fifteen, and
twenty years out. (The research showed that some of the
women who described themselves as "at home," were

actually working part-time or doing work on a freelance basis.)

The career choices women make when they have children are completely personal and absolutely OK—of course they are!—but they have ramifications. Most notably, these choices tend to slow down career advancement.

Is that bad? We don't think so. It's life. Every choice has a consequence. As a working mother, if you decide to take time off, work fewer hours, or travel less, you gain something of immeasurable value: more time with your children. You also give up something: a spot on the fast track. In business—where bosses are paid to win, with shareholders cheering them on—those spots usually go to the people with the most availability and commitment.

But, you may be asking, what about talent? Doesn't talent matter? Fortunately, the answer is yes, and talent is often the saving grace for women who want to have families and career advancement at the same time. Because if you're a working mother who is really good at your job and you really deliver results, most bosses will give you the flexibility you want and need for your children's sake. But you have to earn that flexibility first— with performance. That takes time, in fact, it could take years, which is too long for many mothers to endure.

And so they drop out, shrinking the pool of promotable women, which is yet another reason why women advance more slowly than men.

Perhaps someday, the nature of work will change in a way that makes it possible for men and women to populate the corporate senior ranks in more equal numbers. Companies can't ever stop trying to make that happen by supporting women with training and opportunities and making sure any gender biases are wiped from the system. Many good companies today have already made enormous strides in creating work environments where women can forge creative part-time working solutions to hold on to their careers while their children are young.

But as long as professional advancement is based to a considerable degree on availability and commitment, and as long as mothers want to spend time with their children, women's careers will always have a different, more circuitous path than men's careers. And believe it or not, lots of working mothers wouldn't have it any other way.

■   ■   ■

42

PAYING BIG-TIME FOR FAILURE

What do you think about the obscene severance packages being handed out to CEOs who have basically failed on the job? As a (small) stockholder and a middle manager who busts his butt for five figures, it drives me crazy.

—MIAMI, FLORIDA

Y ou're not alone, but just make sure you aim your anger in the right direction—and that might not be at the CEOs getting the huge payouts. All they did was say, "Yes, thank you," when offered a big package. Greedy? Maybe. But more often, they are simply the beneficiaries of a common and disturbing dynamic that starts in the boardroom.

Which brings us to the real culprits here: company directors. They're behind many severance pay debacles for one main reason. They messed up succession planning.

Yes, succession planning. It has a lot to do with severance pay. Why? Because many of the "obscene" payout deals that bother you so much weren't created when the errant CEO was fired. They were designed long before, when the new CEO was *hired* from the outside because the board failed, over the course of several years, to develop a pool of internal talent.

Now, internally promoted CEOs don't come cheap. The typical insider tapped for the top job will get a substantial pay increase, hefty rewards tied to performance, a slew of new perks, and a bigger office. But the deal gets much richer when a white knight has to be enticed to gallop in to save the company from itself. The rescuer gets everything an insider gets—plus the guarantee of a big consolation prize even if he or she blows it. And indeed, that last part is usually why the deal gets sealed; without back-end protection, no outsider would touch most of these risky positions.

Not all severance messes are related to outsider CEOs, of course. Sometimes insider CEOs fail and get sent on their way with more money than they appear to deserve. That can be galling too, but the dynamic we're talking about is different. It starts when a board needs a new CEO and looking inward, realizes, oops, we forgot to plan for that. They then contact a headhunter, whose lust for a successful placement is second only to the board's level of panic. The dynamic is complete when a seemingly perfect candidate is located—usually in a wonderful, secure job that he or she has no intention of leaving. Unless, of course, the deal is right.

Case in point is what happened at Hewlett-Packard. Back in 1999, when the board decided to change out its CEO, the lack of internal candidates launched head-hunters on a national search. Soon enough, they found Carly Fiorina successfully toiling away at Lucent Technologies. She was hired amid great fanfare, pried away from her comfortable position with, needless to say, an offer she couldn't refuse.

But as everyone knows, Carly's six-year tenure at HP was fraught with board dissension, so much so that you would think when she was fired, her farewell gift would be modest. At about $40 million, it wasn't, sparking widespread hue and cry, much of it aimed at Carly. But what about HP's board? Without doubt, *they* negotiated the severance payout—and they did so as Carly was walking in the door with trumpets blaring, not as it was slamming behind her with a clunk.

The HP case is hardly unique, although sometimes the ending is happier. Take Ed Breen and Tyco. In 2002, Tyco was hit by a disastrous accounting scandal, and its

CEO was removed. Again, the board turned to head-hunters, who quickly set their sights on Ed, a respected executive at Motorola.

But Ed wasn't going to quit a thriving career at an unsullied company to clean up the chaos at Tyco for a standard-issue deal. No wonder the board felt obligated to back up a Brink's truck (metaphorically, of course) to unload a new compensation package at his doorstep. That package had a big performance component to it, but you can be sure that to make the risk of running Tyco worth Ed's while, it also contained plenty of protection in the event things didn't work out. Fortunately, Ed is doing a good job at Tyco, so the terms of his severance package are a moot point.

So, to get back to your question of what we think of obscene severance packages—look, we think they're terrible. But they're not solely the fault of the CEOs carrying them to the bank. In many cases, they were recruited to risky job situations on terms set by the hiring party.

But too bad they had to be bought in the first place. Too bad boards didn't spend enough energy developing internal candidates. They really have only one job more important than that; coaching and supporting the current CEO.

Unfortunately, this problem will probably only get worse going forward. The reason: the Sarbanes-Oxley

Act has driven many boards into a state of frenzied micromanagement of activities outside their purview. Today, many boards are more concerned with accounting minutiae than people development, including succession planning. What a shame. Boards can't do the work of management. They can only make sure the right management is in place, now and in the future.

So, we're with you on this one. We can't blame you for wanting to scream. The big severance packages awarded to failed CEOs make you question the whole capitalistic system. But should you ever decide to really let it rip, just make sure that if the CEO was an outside recruit, you aim your invective where it belongs—not at the easy target, but the right one.

■   ■   ■

CAREERS

*On Life, Liberty, and the
Pursuit of a Promotion*

Without doubt, the majority of the questions we receive, both by e-mail and in person, are about career management, or put less euphemistically, getting ahead. Some questions concern straightforward blocking-and-tackling issues, such as whether an MBA really matters and how to make an impact in a job interview. But others are more nuanced than that, involving complex life choices and sensitive situations with colleagues and bosses. Regardless, almost all career questions share one characteristic: emotional intensity. The drive to succeed is both deeply powerful and entirely personal. People want to move forward in life and in work—and as we say in the following group of answers—with the right mind-set, there's always a way.

43

WHAT SHOULD I DO WITH
THE REST OF MY LIFE?

I am a student with what may seem like a very big question. How can you figure out what to do with your life? I have read many books and taken part in countless activities to help me decide, but still, I cannot take even the first step of my career journey. Can you help?

—MEDAN, INDONESIA

We can mainly help by telling you that you are not alone.

Many young people feel overwhelmed at the beginning of their careers. They see all their friends and classmates getting great fast-track jobs with big salaries—or at least it seems that way. They hear their parents telling them to work here or there, or get some graduate degree or other. And like you, they read books and take part in programs designed to help them with the "What should

I do with my life?" question—but the abundance of answers only confuses matters more.

It's enough to make you panic, which sort of sounds like your state of affairs. And that's OK; it's natural. But it won't really help you move forward.

For that, you have to come to terms with the fact that most careers are not launched by a grand decision about where you want to end up and a clever game plan on how to get you there. No, most careers are iterative. They start with one somewhat appealing job—that is, a job that feels like it *might* be a pretty good match for your skills, interests, and goals. That job typically ends up being not exactly right, so it leads to a job that has a somewhat better fit, which leads to yet another job with an even better fit. And so on and on, until one day—often years from the starting line—you find yourself in the job you have actually been waiting for all your life, the one that gives you meaning and purpose. The one you wished you had known about back when you started but *couldn't*—simply because you hadn't started working yet.

But you know what? Even that "perfect" job will not be without its trials and tribulations. You may be at it for six months and then get a lousy new boss. Or your company may be acquired and your job may change or go away entirely. And your journey will need to start again.

Our point is, careers are long and unpredictable. They are rarely linear. They zig and zag, stop and start, and take many unexpected twists and turns. Hard work and talent matter, and luck will play a role too.

The key for you at this point is just to start. Learn about growing companies, emerging market trends, influential people, and new cultural phenomena. Talk with people in different professions and with varied life stories. Go on interviews. Ask questions. Mull it all over, with both your head and your heart. And incidentally, the latter will probably tell you at least as much as the former.

Then act—take a job. Remember, it doesn't have to be *the* job. It just needs to be a job that feels good enough to get you going.

The job that *calls* you—the career you were meant for—will come. And it will be part of a life journey that you will follow, like most people, one step at a time.

■   ■   ■

44

PICKING THE RIGHT PATH

I am seventeen years old and preparing for university. I am thinking of taking Portuguese, but in your opinion, what language should I learn to succeed in the world of business? And what fields of study hold the most potential?

—TÁBOR, CZECH REPUBLIC

You're onto something with Portuguese, since it will give you a leg up in several markets with good potential, such as Brazil and some emerging African nations. But for our money, Chinese is the language to learn. In the span of your career, China could become the second largest economy in the world. Any European who can do business there with the speed and intimacy that fluency affords will be way ahead of the game.

As for what to study, if you want to be where the action is now and for the next several decades, learn everything you can about the confluence of three fields: biotechnology, information technology, and nanotechnology. For the foreseeable future, the therapies, machines, devices, and other products and services that these fields bring to market will revolutionize society—and business.

That said, when it comes to picking an educational field and ultimately a career, absolutely nothing beats pursuing the path that truly fascinates your brain, engages your energy, and touches your soul. Whatever you do, do what turns your crank. Otherwise your job will always just be work, and how dreary is that?

■   ■   ■

45

I AM WHO I AM

I have achieved a lot as a leader and still want to grow and move on to more challenging positions, but I fail to make an impact at interviews. I always think I am right for the job, but the right answers don't come to me until the interview is over. Your advice?

—JOHANNESBURG, SOUTH AFRICA

Your question reminds us of the time one of us was part of a hiring process where a highly qualified young job candidate strutted into the room and started his interview with the words, "So, let me get this straight. Do you ask me questions in this event, or do I ask you?" His bravado, needless to say, did not exactly win over any hearts.

You don't have a bravado problem—quite the opposite. But it sounds as if you're not winning over any hearts, either. We would guess that's because you're too tied up trying to win over brains with perfectly crafted answers.

That's off track. Your résumé should speak for your credentials. Of course, you can use the interview to elaborate or fill in any blanks on your expertise. But based on your question, it seems more important that you show your potential boss who you really are. That is, a leader who cares about his work and his team passionately. A colleague who can laugh, listen, and worry. A real person with outside interests and friends, maturity and self-awareness, and the ability to connect emotionally.

Indeed, in any interview, your best selling point can be your authenticity. So, stop performing, and be yourself. The positive impact you long for is probably right inside you, if only you'll let it out.

■   ■   ■

46

DOES AN MBA REALLY MATTER?

Over the years, I have noticed that people with an MBA, irrespective of the providing institute and with less experience and less salubrious CVs than myself, land bigger jobs, especially in the top-level executive and leadership positions. This puzzles me. What is it in an MBA that qualifies a graduate to be an automatic winner?

—DURBAN, SOUTH AFRICA

There is no question that an MBA puts a stamp of approval on your forehead. People like credentials, and although some MBAs have more prestige than others, any MBA separates its owner from the pack. A puzzling phenomenon to you, maybe, but nothing new.

But you have to understand something—the impact of an MBA is really good for only a year or so. It helps a graduate get a higher starting salary or land a better job out of the gate, or both. And it creates something of a halo effect. MBAs are presumed to be intelligent and capable; their bosses watch them hopefully and, in many cases, give them extra opportunities to contribute and grow.

In short order, however, an MBA's *performance* kicks in, and in the vast majority of organizations, that is all that comes to matter. The MBA excels or sinks—and the advanced degree becomes forgotten either way. In business, your only real credential, ultimately, is your results.

So, when you see those MBAs around you who appear to be "automatic winners," look beyond their diplomas. We would bet that they are doing a lot more than carrying around a piece of paper. Most likely, they are overdelivering on performance and buying into the values of the company, demonstrating them with their everyday behaviors. On top of that, they are very probably exuding a positive, can-do attitude, taking on tough challenges with a healthy mixture of optimism and realism. Finally, they are almost certainly making the people around them look good too, by sharing credit and building the team. In other words, we would bet they're moving the company forward in some meaningful way. They're making a difference.

Don't get us wrong. We're definitely not discouraging anyone from getting an MBA. It's a credential with heft—it does help critical thinking and introduce you to important managerial concepts best taught in a classroom by a smart professor and debated by high-powered peers. It does get you a better starting salary and more early visibility. But an MBA's leg up lasts for only a finite period, after which performance takes precedent.

So, look again. The "automatic winners" you see around you probably aren't automatic at all. They're successful not just because of a credential they received graduation day, but because of their performance ever since.

■   ■   ■

47

DEAR GRADUATE

As an ambitious twenty-two-year-old readying to enter the corporate world, how can I quickly distinguish myself as a winner?

—CORVALLIS, OREGON

First of all, forget some of the most basic habits you learned in school. Once you are in the real world— and it doesn't make any difference if you are twenty-two or sixty-two, starting your first job or your fifth—the way to get ahead is to overdeliver.

Look, for years, you've been taught the virtues of meeting specific expectations. And you've been trained that it's an A-plus performance to fully answer every question the teacher asks.

Those days are over. To get an A-plus in business, you have to expand the organization's expectations of you and then exceed them, and you have to fully answer every question the "teacher" asks, *plus* a slew of questions he or she didn't even think of.

Your goal, in other words, should be to make your bosses smarter, your team more effective, and the whole company more competitive because of your energy, creativity, and insights.

And you thought school was hard!

But don't panic. Just get in there and start thinking big. If your boss asks you for a report on the outlook for one of your company's products over the next year, you can be sure she already has a solid sense of the answer. So, go beyond being the grunt assigned to confirm her hunch. Do the extra research, legwork, and data crunching to give her something that really expands her thinking—an analysis, for instance, of how the entire industry might play out over the next three years. What new companies and products might emerge? What technologies could change the game? Could someone, perhaps your own company, move production to China?

In other words, give your boss something that shocks and awes her, something new and interesting that she can report to *her* bosses. In time, those kinds of ideas will move the company forward and you upward.

But be careful. People who strive to overdeliver can quickly self-destruct if their big, wonderful, exciting suggestions are seen by others as unfettered braggadocio or not-so-subtle ladder scaling—or both.

That's right—personal ambition can backfire.

Now, we're not saying to curb yours. In fact, you should have it—have tons. But the minute you wear career lust on your sleeve, you run the risk of alienating people, in particular your peers. They will soon come to doubt the motives of your hard work. They will see any comments you make about, say, how the team could operate better, as political jockeying. And they will eventually see you as a striver, and in the long run, that's a label that all the A-plus performing in the world can't overcome.

So, by all means, overdeliver—but keep your desire to distinguish yourself as a winner to yourself. You'll become one faster.

■   ■   ■

48

BIG COMPANY OR START-UP?

Next spring, I will graduate from a great college, single and basically debt free. Right now, I have two options. I can return to the big company where I had a summer internship doing work I sort of liked with people I sort of liked. Or I can join a start-up with three friends, which is a long shot but could be a blast. What should I do?

—PALO ALTO, CALIFORNIA

At age twenty-one, with not a mortgage or student loan in sight, why would you ever, ever sign up to huddle in a corporate cubicle where you will do work you *sort of* like? To make your parents happy? To look good to your classmates? Don't do that! In fact, in your situation, don't even be worried if the people who love you most hear about your new job and react by saying, "You're doing *what*?"

If there was ever a time to take chances, explore options, and swing for the fences, it is now. You can be cautious later, when you have an apartment in the city and a house in the country and two kids' tuitions to pay. And your spouse loves luxury travel, expensive paintings, or most frightening of all, horses.

Right now, you're as free as you will ever be. Plus, you've got a very nice credential hanging on your wall in your college degree. So take full advantage of what you've got: the open-mindedness to experiment, the capacity to live cheaply, and the permission most cultures grant young people to take risks and fail a few times.

These gifts probably won't come your way again. Enjoy them!

■   ■   ■

49

IT STARTS WITH SELF-CONFIDENCE

I am a young person, not long out of school, filled with ambition, creative ideas, and a burning desire to achieve a lot of things in my life, but one thing holds me back: fear of blowing it. How can I get some nerve?

—JOHANNESBURG, SOUTH AFRICA

You don't really need "nerve" exactly—you need self-confidence. Without it, you're going nowhere, but you seem to know that already.

Look, only you know why and how self-confidence has eluded you so far. Perhaps you weren't born with much, as there does indeed seem to be a genetic component to it. But by far, self-confidence is a developed trait. Some people get it at their mother's knee, where they first hear the happy news that their every bright comment qualifies them for the Nobel Prize, or that they're taller, more clever, and certainly better looking than every other child on the block. Others get it from great grades that set them apart, or sports at school, whether they score goals or get elected captain.

But there are no rules about where self-confidence begins. We know a twenty-seven-year-old entrepreneur from Slovenia who picked up self-confidence by watching his father struggle to launch a little machine tool company in 1991, literally just days after the country won independence from Yugoslavia. Today, this gutsy young man, fresh off an MBA in the United States, is in the midst of launching a global technology company of his own and sees no limits to his future.

We also know a successful New York mutual fund manager who got his first big dose of self-confidence as an adolescent, when he learned to pilot a small boat alone and spent a summer reeling in bluefish and striped bass in the rough seas of Cape Cod Bay. "After that," he told us, "I thought I could do anything."

Could he? Absolutely not. Through his long career, this mutual fund manager would tell you he has blown it many times. He started a communications company his senior year in college, grew it to a hundred employees and $40 million in sales, then lost it in a painful, protracted legal battle with a former partner. Several years later, he tried to start a consulting firm, which survived six months. But if those incidents spawned fear, this entrepreneur's deep reservoir of self-confidence overcame it every time.

You need to start creating that kind of reservoir for yourself, even if it is from scratch.

How? Not with grandiose plans concocted to catapult you to fame and fortune and quash your fear of failure once and for all. Too many people believe that one big, public success will solve their self-confidence problems forever.

That only happens in the movies.

In real life, the opposite strategy is what works. Call it the "small victories" approach.

To begin, set a realistic goal, be it at work or home. Keep this goal attainable and contained; don't overextend your expectations of yourself the first time out.

Then achieve that goal and feel good. You should.

Next, set a slightly larger goal, something somewhat bolder and enough of a stretch to put you slightly out of your comfort zone. Achieve that goal and feel even better. And so forth until you're in a slow and steady forward march, building self-confidence step-by-step.

And it will build. One of us (Jack) delivered his first speech forty-odd years ago. It was a panic-inducing, awkward, heavily rehearsed event, practiced in front of the mirror for weeks in hopes of keeping his stammer in check, and then read from carefully typed sheets with all the ease of a man in a straitjacket. The actual talk took just fifteen minutes; however, they were (reportedly) the longest ever lived.

But there's nothing more effective than tackling a challenge incrementally, growing and learning each time. After delivering speeches for decades to all kinds of audiences, today, for Jack, answering questions without notes in front of thousands of people is the opposite of nerve-racking; it's fun.

Now, without doubt, you will screw up along the way as you try to build your self-confidence. Not every one of Jack's speeches was better than the one before it, and it was a long time before giving them became fully enjoyable. But when your small victory turns out to be a small defeat, do not revert to fear mode. Go deep into that reservoir, understand what went wrong, set another goal, and start again.

The process won't ever really end. As time goes on, your goals will just keep getting bigger and bigger. And failure, which will also occur on occasion, will come to feel like less and less of a thing to fear.

In time, you will discover that all failing really does is teach you something you needed to know—so you can regroup and stretch again, with ever more . . . nerve.

■   ■   ■

50

THE TRUTH ABOUT MENTORING

Career development articles always say the same thing: "Find a good mentor." It makes sense too, since mentors have been pivotal in the lives of so many people, opening up whole worlds of knowledge and experience. So, what advice do you have for getting someone like Bill Clinton or Warren Buffett to meet for even thirty minutes with a twenty-four-year-old?

—NEW YORK, NEW YORK

Our advice would be that you are barking up the wrong tree. No doubt both Mr. Clinton and Mr. Buffett would give you profound insights into how to succeed in life and work. But a mentor isn't a luminary with thirty minutes to spare. Frankly, a mentor isn't even a VIP executive at your own company with an hour alloted just for you every other week.

Or it might be, as long as you have lots of other mentors too. And that's our point. The single, looming, all-important mentor—as you point out, the Holy Grail of career development advice—is just so limiting! You want *everyone* you meet along the path of your career to be a mentor in some way or another, teaching you whatever he or she knows that you don't.

Many companies, of course, don't exactly approach mentoring with this mind-set. Instead, they sponsor formal mentoring programs in which bright young things are officially linked with older-and-wiser types for regularly scheduled meetings. Too often, such manufactured relationships are good mainly for directions to the lunchroom and tips on how to navigate the company's benefits system. Devoid of any real chemistry or work-related meaning, they usually devolve into nothingness pretty quickly.

By contrast, the best mentoring relationships are informal, forged not just with random higher-ups, but with peers and subordinates too—that is, with anyone who can expand your knowledge and way of thinking. These relationships, inside your organization and out, within your functional area or not, can last weeks or a lifetime. They can grow into friendships or be purely functional. Either way, they are about learning at every opportunity—from every person willing to teach you.

We're not saying you shouldn't try to get on the calendars of the world's leading lights—more power to you—but we are suggesting there might be a better long-term use of your time. Look for good ideas everywhere. Every time you find one, you've got yourself another mentoring experience.

■   ■   ■

51

THE BAD BOSS NO-BRAINER

What's better: to work for a bad boss at a good company, or a good boss at a weak company?

We've gotten this question several times while traveling around the world, and we have been amazed at how split audiences seem on the answer. Amazed, because to us this is an absolute no-brainer. If you had to pick between these options, by all means, work for the good company!

Here's our reasoning. If you truly are at a good company, its leaders will eventually find the bad boss and get him or her out. That can take time—months, or even a year or more. In that case, you might even be rewarded with a promotion for having delivered results during your ordeal. After all, everyone's been there at some point in his or her career, toiling for someone moody, mean, or just plain incompetent.

But even if you're not promoted for your "hardship duty," you will still be better off for having endured. You will be able to stay where you are in the good company with a new and better boss or move sideways to a fresh opportunity. Remember: any experience you get at a good company, around smart people, is worthwhile, and a good company's reputation gives you an excellent career credential down the road, if you need it.

Now think about the other scenario. Without question, having a good boss is one of life's best experiences. Good bosses can make work fun, meaningful, and all those warm, fuzzy things. Good bosses can make work feel like a home away from home. They can make your team feel like a family. In some cases, they can even make you feel like you've found a long lost friend or finally gotten parental approval.

But the good boss–weak company dynamic is a velvet coffin. All bosses eventually depart—moved up, out, or sideways. And someday your good boss will leave you too. In fact, good bosses in weak companies are especially vulnerable to change, because they have the extra stress of "protecting" their people from the impact of the company's larger problems. This burden can wear them out or make them political pariahs or both. Either way, in time, they go.

In other words, the great feeling you get from working for a good boss in a weak company is only temporary. Your boss will leave, but the weak company will still be there, and you won't be able to do a thing about it. You'll be trapped. Getting a new job after you've worked at a company with a mediocre or poor reputation is hard. It's almost as if you're tainted.

In some ways, then, this question comes down to a choice between short- and long-term gains. In the short term, working for a bad boss, even in a good company, can be a living hell. But in the long term, when the boss is gone, at least you'll have opportunity to move on.

Working for a good boss in the short term, of course, can be thoroughly enjoyable, even when the company is collapsing around you. Long-term, however, those happy vibes will come back to bite you. Your boss will be gone, and all you'll have is a second-rate credential and nice memories.

By all means, do your career a favor and get your memories elsewhere.

■　■　■

52

WE'VE JUST BEEN ACQUIRED
AND I HATE IT

My small company was recently acquired by a global corporation, and I can't stand what's going on. In trying to make us just like them, the new owners are killing what made us worth acquiring in the first place. I love my old company, but I am thinking about getting out of here. Should I?

—ATLANTA, GEORGIA

Your language says it all—"the new owners," you say, and "my old company." You sound just like the bane of every acquiring company in the history of mergers. You're a resister, and if you don't change your ways, you probably won't last anyway.

Now, we definitely don't want to belittle how hard it is to go through an acquisition. When your company is bought or folded into another entity, even as a "merger of equals," it can absolutely feel like a death has occurred.

Every work relationship you've had is ruptured. Every achievement you've posted is pretty much forgotten. The future looks very uncertain, and often pretty grim. Overall, for people at the company being bought, acquisitions usually feel absolutely awful.

But you have to face reality. When good companies do acquisitions, the *buyers* feel pretty terrific. They're excited, filled with optimism, and dreaming about all the opportunities that their new purchase will bring. (After all, they've usually paid a lot for it!) One of those opportunities is the chance to find great people within the acquired company. In fact, smart acquirers are thinking, "We've just landed a whole new pool of players to choose from."

As the new owners go about picking the best and brightest from the combined teams, they are looking for two things: talent and commitment. But make no mistake—they want those two traits *blended* in each individual. Talent alone is not enough. In fact, if there is one thing we have learned from working through and watching hundreds of M & A events, it is that companies will always choose to keep and promote people with buy-in over resisters, even if the resisters have more brains. No acquirer in the world wants someone around who is whining and moaning about the "good old days." It doesn't make any difference how much they know.

The bottom line is: acquiring managers believe that if you're not for the deal, you're against it. And even if you think you are keeping your objections hidden, the new owners can probably feel your negativity. And if that's the case, the decision to stay or leave may not actually be yours much longer.

Look, change is hard. But in business, it's inevitable. Your best bet is to bid a fond farewell to the past—it's over. Find a way to like your new boss, adopt the values and practices of your new organization, and embrace the future, whatever it holds.

If you can't do that—that is, if you really cannot accept that the new company is now *your* company—then you had better leave. Resisters never get what they want. The old days won't come again, and in pining for them, you actually number your own.

■   ■   ■

53

FROM HERO TO ZERO

Up until the age of sixteen, I won at everything: sport, academics, and I even got the girl. Not unnaturally, this success bred a feeling of confidence in my own abilities, and that remains with me to this day, at the age of thirty-two. But something clicked starting when I was seventeen, and it has since developed into a damaging trend—people in a position of power or authority consistently work against me. Save the occasional mentor who says I remind them of their "younger selves," I seem destined to stall on the corporate ladder or be removed. Is the college hero destined for zero?

—LONDON, ENGLAND

We're actually optimistic for you—because it is a rare jerk (for lack of a more politically correct term) who recognizes that he is a jerk. Usually, people in your position blame others for their stalled careers; you seem to understand your own complicity in events. And most hopeful of all, you appear to be looking for a solution.

If we had to guess, your main sin is a very common one with young people who get on a winning streak—you didn't grow, you *swelled*. People who swell develop all sorts of unappealing behaviors. They're arrogant, especially toward their peers and subordinates. They hoard credit and belittle the efforts of others, don't share ideas except to show them off, and don't listen very well, if at all. Bosses can spot these team-killing behaviors a mile away, and so it is no wonder that those with "power and authority" around you, as you put it, have consistently worked against you. You may be very smart and deliver stellar results on the job, but your swollen personality is the kind that undermines the morale in any organization and ultimately can really damage performance.

But good for you for seeing that you are headed for a fall. That's the first step toward getting your career restarted. Unfortunately, you may not be able to do so at your current company. You've probably burned too many bridges already. So, here is what we suggest. Starting today, take an inventory of your negative behaviors. Explaining that you are hoping to change your dysfunctional ways, ask your bosses, peers, and subordinates to give you brutally candid feedback, anonymously or in writing if that makes it easier for them. Be prepared for a terrible awakening, as people pour out your shortcomings with lots of stored-up resentment.

After you've processed what you've learned, you can attempt a recovery at your current company. Who knows—people may be so delighted with your new humility and desire to improve that they will be willing to give you a second chance. It is more likely, however, that you will need to move on, as some organizational wounds never heal. And it might also be better too for you to get a fresh start at a place where an awful reputation doesn't precede you at every turn.

Your new job search, of course, will probably be hobbled by lousy references. You will be noted for your high IQ, perhaps, but also for your arrogance. There is only one way to handle that problem—with total candor. Tell prospective employers that you swelled instead of grew because of your early successes, but you've learned the hard lesson of that mistake and are eager to make amends in a new position. Assure them that you are committed to being a team player, and that you will frequently seek feedback in order to stay on the straight and narrow.

Your past failings will hurt you. There's no sugarcoating that. But eventually, a good employer will be impressed with your early record of success, your obvious talent, plus your newfound candor and maturity. Good luck starting over. We'll bet on you.

■   ■   ■

54

AM I AN ENTREPRENEUR?

I am currently a consultant with a small organizational development firm, but I dream about starting my own business. How do I know if I have what it takes to be an entrepreneur? I always experience such conflicting emotions when it comes to this issue.

—JOHANNESBURG, SOUTH AFRICA

Your conflicting emotions concern you; they concern us too—a lot. Being an entrepreneur *without* ambivalence is a tough road. It's got to be twice as tough *with* it!

Still, the idea intrigues you enough to ask what it takes to be an entrepreneur. Your question alone proves you understand a fundamental truth about business: entrepreneurs really are a breed apart from company types. Incidentally, there's no value judgment in that statement. Both kinds of lives can be totally fulfilling. But they're different.

So, here are four questions. If you answer yes to them

all, forget your mixed emotions and get out there on your
own. You've got the makings of an entrepreneur.

1. **Do you have a great new idea that makes your
product or service compelling to customers in a
way no competitor can match?** Sometimes people are
attracted to the "lifestyle" of entrepreneurs—control,
autonomy, the possibility of huge wealth, and all that—
but they don't really have the blockbuster idea to make
it actually occur. Real entrepreneurs not only have a
unique value proposition for the marketplace, they are
madly in love with it. They passionately believe they
have discovered the greatest thing since gravity, and
now all they have to do is sell it to the whole wide waiting world.

2. **Do you have the stamina to hear "no" over and
over again and keep smiling?** Entrepreneurs spend
a lot of their time asking (and sometimes even begging) venture capitalists, banks, and other investors for
money. Often they get a stick in the eye. Now, no one
likes getting rejected, but entrepreneurs have the resil-
ience not to be daunted by it. The best of the lot even
get *energized* by the experience; hearing no only makes
them get out there and sell their idea even harder.

3. **Do you hate uncertainty?** If so, stop reading here.
Entrepreneurs spend more time in blind alleys than

stray cats, if not chasing dollars, chasing new technology or service concepts, not to mention everything else they need to build a business. If not in blind alleys, they're aboard a leaky boat on choppy seas—or put more plainly, they are often running out of money while betting on the unknown. If you're an entrepreneur, that actually sounds like, well, fun.

4. **Do you have the personality to attract bright people to chase your dream with you?** Early on as an entrepreneur, of course, you may work alone. But with any kind of success, you are going to need to hire great people whom you can't pay very much. To do that, you need the special talent of making people love your dream as much as you do. You need the ability to convert employees into true believers.

We certainly don't want to discourage anyone from starting his or her own business. The free markets depend on entrepreneurs; they're the lifeblood of healthy economies everywhere. Just know, however, that going out on your own is a radical departure from any company job you've ever had.

Stay put if that worries you—and get going if it excites you to no end.

■ ■ ■

55

A CASE OF EMBEDDED REPUTATION?

I'm really confused. I received my annual bonus today, and it is 10 percent lower than last year. Here's the problem. I was hired a year ago as a secretary at my company. But, attending school part time, I received a degree in public relations, and six months ago was promoted to a higher grade as a staff member in the Communications Department. I have met my targets, received letters of commendation, and have a heavier workload than before. Still—less bonus! What should I do?

—JOHANNESBURG, SOUTH AFRICA

Your letter leaves out two critical pieces of information when it comes to making sense of bonuses: how did the overall company do this year, and how did your department perform? If the answer to either of those questions is "worse than last year," then the reason for your 10 percent decrease could be right under your nose.

Another possibility could be a good old-fashioned bureaucratic screwup. Your old boss and your new boss might not have exchanged notes about your pay, or the HR department may have missed a beat when you changed positions. It happens.

But there is a third possibility, and definitely one to think hard about if your company and department did well over the past year: You may have hit your targets, but your performance is a *relative* thing. It can be (and probably is) measured relative to what was expected of you and to the performance of other members of the team. It is possible you've done well enough to receive positive feedback, but not as well as hoped, or not as well as a number of your coworkers.

There is, of course, only one way to find out what's going on, and that is to have a candid conversation with your boss. Make an appointment, and calmly ask her to explain your bonus. Your main goal with this talk is to *learn*. So listen more than talk, and by all means, do it soon. Don't ever let confusion fester. In time, it will only grow into anger.

One last point here, and it is a broader one for anyone who has gotten a degree while working at a company. In our experience, once you've bettered yourself with education at night or part-time, you're much better off moving on to another organization. People tend to have what we call an "embedded reputation" at their companies. A degree just never seems to change that, even if your work improves. If you want real bang for your education's buck, take your new credential elsewhere, where it stands a much better chance of making you look as good as you intended it to.

■   ■   ■

56

WHY CAN'T I GET HIRED?

I currently run a small management consulting firm in "survivalist mode"—in other words, it's failing due to lack of financial resources. A few months ago, I decided to quit the business and started sending out my résumé for executive positions. The response has been discouraging, to put it mildly. Do you think the problem is with my résumé, or that maybe I am not presenting myself convincingly in interviews? In short, how should I market myself to get out of my bind?

—JOHANNESBURG, SOUTH AFRICA

Let's face reality. Consultants usually have a very easy time landing new jobs. They're typically well educated, have some degree of sophisticated critical thinking skills, and can boast of both broad industry experience and familiarity with cutting-edge management tools. The fact that you aren't being snatched up by some company out there suggests something might not only be wrong with your résumé or your presentation during interviews—something might be wrong with your expectations.

Have you considered that you could be shooting too high? After all, your main credential—or your most recent one, at least—is the firm that you run, and it's in trouble. Obviously, failure is not a good sign to any potential employer. Companies are looking for winners.

So, what can you do to get out of your "bind," as you so aptly call it? Our first piece of advice would be to actively look for, and be eager to interview for, lower-level jobs than you have been considering to this point. The hard reality of the situation is that you may not be able to reenter the workforce in an executive position. You may need to get your foot in the door simply as a team member or individual contributor with no managerial responsibilities whatsoever. That may not feel great for your ego or your pocketbook, but if you're good, your career should leap forward quickly as you demonstrate what you've got.

Along with shooting a bit lower, a second piece of advice is to market yourself with total candor. On both your résumé and in interviews, do not try to sugarcoat the fact that your consulting firm is not making it. Don't blame "lack of financial resources," as if the firm's failure was out of your hands. *You* were the boss; *you* weren't able to raise enough seed capital, or get enough clients, or serve them economically enough, to make money. *Own* the firm's collapse. Say what you think you did wrong and what you will do differently in the future to be a winner. Describe what you learned from the experience, how it made you a better businessperson—more insightful, more decisive, and so on. Your résumé tells a lot about you, but your honesty and authenticity—and your desire to start over, only better—will impress potential employers more than anything else you can say.

Finally, stay positive. The process of landing a job out of a bad situation usually takes longer than you'd like and is more daunting too. But frustration or anger—or any negative emotion—will only make the search worse for you. You'll feel enervated, and your demeanor, no matter how hard you try to hide it, will make you less attractive to companies. So, do whatever it takes to draw on your reserves of self-confidence. Lean on friends and family in private, and then get out there and play to win—upbeat, candid to your toes, and willing to reboot your career with a job where you can demonstrate all the untapped potential you've got.

■   ■   ■

57

THEY'RE TELLING YOU SOMETHING

I have an ethical dilemma. I am an in-house consultant at a manufacturing company, where I use conceptual tools to help improve processes. I have noticed, however, that company executives do not find my work useful or important for results. Should I leave the company, thereby being disloyal to my manager, or stay, knowing that my work might never be properly recognized?

—SÃO PAULO, BRAZIL

You don't have an ethical problem. You have a classic career problem, and its solution is straightforward: you need to get out.

Look, you're at a company where the work you do is not valued. We're afraid that it doesn't really make any difference if you are right or wrong. Your work could have the potential to unlock untold profits. But if your bosses fundamentally don't think it matters, you will be shouting into the wind forever. Do yourself a favor. Find another place where management will value the conceptual stuff you do. And chances are, the manager you leave behind won't feel you've been disloyal. He knows what's going on—and he'll be happy to replace you with someone more in tune with management's mind-set.

We called your problem "classic," incidentally, because it's so very common. It typically starts as yours did, with an employee's creeping sense that the terrific work he or she is doing doesn't particularly interest the powers that be. The situation quickly spirals down as the employee becomes angry and frustrated and the bosses grow annoyed. As the disconnect widens, the employee's performance usually worsens, and feelings of resentment—on both sides—expand to the breaking point.

Then, boom, the employee is usually canned or quits in a rage. Luckily, it is not too late to avoid that in your case. Make your exit amicable and orderly, which will be good for both the company and your reputation going forward. But do what you need to do soon—move on.

■   ■   ■

58

WELCOME TO THE GOVERNMENT, KID

I am twenty-two years old, straight out of the University of Georgia, where I studied finance and filled my summers with great business internships. I am now on the staff of a U.S. senator, and while the work is fascinating, I am having a hard time adjusting to the public sector mind-set. Any advice?

—WASHINGTON, D.C.

Welcome to the world of politics, where every business value you've been taught over the past couple of years is pretty much null and void. We mean values like clear goal-setting, rewards for achievement, productivity, and speed. Surely your finance professors sang their praises, and your summer bosses did the same. But politics has different values, and your adjustment problem suggests you've begun to discover them.

Don't worry.

Your new job is part of a system that is absolutely essential to the healthy functioning of society. No doubt you felt proud to accept a position in government, and you were right to.

But something's bothering you, and if we had to guess, it's the . . . well, the politics of politics. The bureaucracy. The compromising. The deals, favors, and earmarks. The lack of differentiation and candor. The "I'll scratch your back, you scratch mine" mentality of the whole scene. It's all so uncompetitive, right?

Right—and not changing. Government is filled with the inefficiencies of politics and always will be.

Now, that's OK for some people; they make their careers in government. But given your rapid discomfort, you don't sound like part of that crowd. Your future is in the private sector.

No rush, though. The good news is that a few years in politics can be very good for a business career. Knowing how things get done in government can be very useful in all sorts of situations you may face, especially as you get to more senior levels in a company.

The same, however, can't really be said of the reverse. That is, it's rare that experience in business helps people succeed in government. Yes, capitals everywhere have a smattering of former CEOs in high-ranking roles, but very few of them have achieved great things, to put it mildly.

Why? Who knows for sure, but we'd wager they feel the exact same frustrations you do—only multiplied by a lot.

■ ■ ■

59

KNOWING WHEN TO FOLD 'EM

You make the case that leaders should be candid, and I agree. But what would you advise a middle manager who works in a company where leaders place challenging questions in the "parking lot," rarely answering them, and tend to stunt (or end) the careers of people who keep asking them?

—MINNEAPOLIS, MINNESOTA

Before answering, can we ask you a kind of awful question, with all due respect? Is the problem possibly you? It does happen, now and again, that leaders ignore "challenging questions" because those questions are more annoying than constructive—and the people asking them are too.

If that's you, and you have the self-awareness to accept that unpleasant fact, our only suggestion is to redirect your energies toward real work—or *you'll* be in the parking lot before long.

But let's assume that's not you, and that your questions are meaningful, if maybe a bit touchy. In that case, you're in one of two situations, neither of them optimal but both actionable.

It could be you have a boss problem—that is, your boss is something of a jerk and can't handle open dialogue, particularly if it is potentially contentious. In that case, if you like your job well enough, your best bet is to wait it out for a while. In time, most good organizations find such stultifying idea-blockers and move them elsewhere or out.

On the other hand, you could have a culture problem, that is, the leadership of the organization in general does not relish constructive curiosity as a way of life. In that case, you have a question to ask yourself. Does your job have enough upside to live with this objectionable downside?

We are not trying to lead the witness—the answer could be yes.

Take the case of a friend of ours. About twelve years ago, he became logistics director at a small consulting firm. Since then, the firm has fared pretty well, but its three partners have steadfastly remained opaque. Employees never know what the partners are thinking about the firm's direction—do they want to build or flip?—or how they rate each person's performance. The result is a constant sense of anxiety and basic confusion about strategy and resource allocation.

Our friend, however, has no plans to leave. He makes a good salary, for one, and he enjoys a short commute. The work is interesting enough, he says, and he likes most of his colleagues. Yes, the leadership's lack of candor drives him nuts—"intermittently," as he puts it—and he feels certain that it has hindered the firm's growth by "some significant amount."

But, as he says, "I've traded an OK quality of work for a great quality of life. A good deal, if you ask me."

Like our friend, you too can stay and make peace with your situation. Or you know you have reached your limit and start to look for another job. To fall between these options—to hang around and complain under your breath—is a fast track to probably the worst workplace hell imaginable: victimhood. People with this self-infliction conceive of themselves as vanquished heroes. Their bosses see them as energy-sapping boors. Do not go there!

Only you know what deal you will ultimately make. Just be sure you make a choice—one way or another.

■   ■   ■

60

ARE YOU A BOSS HATER?

My wife and I regularly see incompetence, tolerance
for stupid decision making, and outright unprofession-
alism at the Fortune 500 companies where we work.
Why is it so hard to find a manager that you can respect, follow, and learn something from?

—BARRINGTON, ILLINOIS

It's not hard. But it does require a certain mind-set—
one you may have difficulty finding in yourself. If so,
you're not alone.

Every week, in fact, we receive several e-mails that
sound like yours. The wording and details are different, of course, but the underlying question is always the
same: Why am I the only person at my company who
gets it?

Now, we realize there are days when it can feel as
if everyone around you is inept. Companies, after all,
are comprised of people, and people can screw up, re-

ward mediocrity, play politics, and otherwise commit a myriad of organizational sins. But the "everyone's dumb but me" perspective is dangerous. Not only is it a career killer, it's simply not right. How do you explain the thriving, creative financial services industry? Or the envelope-pushing genius of the life sciences field? The fact is: too many companies perform well every day, inventing, making, selling, and distributing millions of products and services and returning billions in profits, for every manager out there to be a total nincompoop. It just can't be.

Which is why we suggest that you reflect on your own mind-set, looking for an attitude that might explain your gloomy view of the working world. To be direct, we are wondering if you might be a boss hater.

Now, very few people would ever identify themselves as boss haters—they usually see themselves as noble victims, "speaking truth to power," as it were. Forget that line. Boss haters are a real breed. It doesn't matter where they work—big corporations, small family firms, partnerships, nonprofits, newspapers, or government agencies. Boss haters enter into any authority relationship with barely repressed cynicism and ingrained negativity toward "the system." And even though the reasons behind their attitude may be varied, from upbringing to personality to political bent, boss haters are unified in their inability to see the value in any person above them in a hierarchy.

Interestingly, the boss haters in any organization tend to find one another, and once in numbers, they usually become quite outspoken. Boss haters also tend to be on the high IQ side. It's unfortunate, really. Because instead of using their intelligence to look for new ideas to improve the way work is done, boss haters focus laserlike on all of the organization's flaws and the sheer, incomprehensible idiocy of the higher-ups.

Of course, due to their general intelligence, some boss haters do get ahead—briefly. But more often, the organization feels their vibe, and bosses respond in kind with distancing, or worse.

Now, maybe you're not a boss hater. But the sweeping nature of your question pretty much tests that notion. We suggest, then, that you test yourself. Could it really be that every single boss you've encountered has a problem?

Or is the problem something you could fix—just by opening up your mind?

■ ■ ■

61

LOOKING FOR A SECOND ACT

I'm fifty-eight, and about two years ago I took a forced "early retirement" from my middle management job in sales. Since then, I've had real trouble getting back in the game, despite sending out tons of résumés and leaning hard on my networking "buddies." I have a lot to offer, and I'm not ready to call it quits. What next?

—KANSAS CITY, MISSOURI

Having exhausted traditional companies that obviously find you too old, too unfamiliar with the ways of the new world, or otherwise too problematic to bring on board, you've got at least one option remaining: find a company where hiring you represents absolutely zero risk.

You need, in other words, a job where the compensation is entirely variable—you get paid on commission and receive little or no salary. Yes, most of those kinds of positions will feel like nursery school to an old sales hand like yourself. But with your experience and ambition, you should be skipping grades pretty quickly. All you need is that first door, which we assure you will swing open when you say the magic words to an employer: "Give me a shot—I'm free."

■ ■ ■

62

CAN YOU HEAR IT?

There seems to be an explosion in executive coaching recently. Does it really work?

—EDINBURGH, SCOTLAND

Generally, yes. Its value depends, of course, on the quality of the coach. This is a field where there is no specific training and accreditation only for those who seek it out. There are certainly some charlatans out there who simply tell you what you want to hear, or don't have much feel for leadership, never having done it themselves. Obviously, they're useless.

But good executive coaches can provide a truly important service. They can look you in the eye and tell you what no one else will, especially if you're the boss. Messages like: You don't listen carefully enough, or you're too much of a loner, or you kiss up to the board but too often bully your people. They can tell you that you rely too much on the advice of one employee who really isn't very smart, or basically any number of other unpleasant messages that take real guts to deliver.

The challenge is for you to hear them. Because at the end of the day, the ultimate value of executive coaching—done right—is only as big or small as your ability to receive it.

■   ■   ■

PRIVATELY HELD

On Working for the Family

B efore we wrote *Winning*, we would typically answer questions about privately held enterprises with a pass. We believed that such companies, often characterized by complex family relationships and absence of conventional "due process," were out of our area of expertise. But since the book's publication, we've been delighted to discover just how useful *Winning* has been to many private companies, and we've started to spend more time with their owners and managers. Yes, private companies have their own unique set of issues. But as the following (short) section of this book shows, they share one goal with the corporate world, and sometimes with even more passion: to create a better company for the next generation.

63

BUT WHAT ABOUT TOMORROW?

I work for my father, the founder of a very successful family business with a terrific management team. The problem is that my father, while a superb leader, has no succession plan. But for the sake of the company and our kids' future, we need one. How can I approach him about this without looking like I want to "get" the company for personal gain?

—CHICAGO, ILLINOIS

First things first. You don't necessarily need a succession plan. You *want* one.

And for that matter, your father—superb leader that he is—may very well have a plan. He's just not telling you.

Either way, you're getting a taste of what it feels like to work at a regular old public company, where succession plans are usually tightly held information until quite late in the game. And yet somehow, those companies still manage to move forward from one CEO to the next, and their executives manage to plan for their kids' futures. With less information, they just end up having to use their judgment.

Yes, life would be easier for you, and for *all* CEO candidates, if they knew more about the future earlier. But we can think of at least three reasons why it so rarely happens that way.

First, people develop at different rates. A possible successor who starts in a blaze of glory might fade over time, and a slow starter might take off. A CEO needs several years at least to see candidates in many jobs and differing economic environments before making a final call.

Second, making a succession announcement too early can throw a company into disarray if there aren't backup plans to replace the talent that inevitably leaves when a new CEO is picked. Such plans take time to put in place.

Finally, if a CEO is doing a terrific job and enjoying himself—like your dad, by the way—he has no interest in becoming a premature lame duck.

We suggest, then, that you give your father the benefit of the doubt. According to details of your letter that we didn't print at your request, he's quite a man. Your family business is in a brutally competitive industry, but he's led it with insight and skill for decades, and it's thriving. He's built a deep management team and is respected by all. Surely he isn't being a fool about succession. He has a reason you should wait, and if he is the leader he seems to be, you'll understand why in due time.

■   ■   ■

64

THE NITTY-GRITTY ON NEPOTISM

I was recently hired as a manager at a family-owned company. My boss, the vice president of marketing, is the CEO's wife. She never went to college, has no experience in marketing, yet micromanages everyone, including those of us with MBAs. I've just learned that several talented people have quit because of her, and that she fires anyone who disagrees with her, with her husband's full support. Short of quitting, how do I handle nepotism gone awry?

—AUSTIN, TEXAS

Not to be difficult here, but where the heck were you during the hiring process for this job?

We ask because it seems a little late for you to be discovering the kind of information that should be part of everyone's due diligence when considering employment at a family-owned company. Information like: how many cousins want your next promotion, and whether it is fatal—or merely dangerous—to disagree with the CEO's next of kin.

Now, we're not implying that people should avoid working in family-owned companies. These organizations, which make up a significant part of the economy, offer some of the best jobs in business.

But when you decide to work at a family-owned company, you have to realize you are accepting a special deal. And every deal has trade-offs.

With this one, the upside is real. Family-owned companies give you a level of collegiality and informality rarely found in corporate environments, with cultures that are, at their best, personal and warm. Employees can come to feel like family members, not numbers, and managers (like you, for instance) often have direct access to the shareholders and decision makers. You can really feel like you're in the game.

The downside is real too, as you are discovering. Because when you join a family-owned business, especially a small or medium-size one, you very often give up the adjudication process, for lack of a better term, that "enforces" fairness at professionally run organizations. That's not saying that public companies don't have their share of arbitrary or bullying bosses, or that they are devoid of favoritism. But the checks and balances at most public companies, such as employee satisfaction surveys and the "higher authority" of HR, do go a long way in giving employees a sense that there is a way for them to be heard during conflicts.

The only way to handle the absence of adjudication at family companies is to be prepared. Even if things are going well, employees should always have an exit strategy. And if you are considering joining a family company as a CEO, or even as a high-level manager, don't make a move unless you negotiate a severance package up front.

But what about your case? You don't seem to have a contract, and you say you don't want to quit. That means your only choice is, well, to adjust. You have to figure out the best way to work with the CEO's wife. Forget her educational credentials, or lack thereof—she's still your boss. So, slow down your desire to make changes or speak out, and give her a chance to get to know you— and trust you.

Yes, proper due diligence during the hiring process might have raised red flags, and perhaps you could have avoided the mess you're in. But it's too late for that now. The nepotism you're encountering is part of the family-owned deal.

Enjoy its benefits while they last.

■   ■   ■

65

THE CONSEQUENCES OF CASHING OUT

After sixty-one years as a family business, our company was just sold to a $250 million corporation. We will keep our name, operate as an independent business unit, and everyone will keep their jobs. In effect, everything is the same, but we know it's not. How do I, as president, and my employees make the quickest and most appropriate adjustment to our new world?

—BRIDGEPORT, CONNECTICUT

Congratulations . . . and congratulations. The first for the deal itself—you and your top team probably did pretty well cashing out, and you should feel great about the financial rewards of building a company that the market loved.

The second congratulations is for realizing that, even though everything might look the same going forward, nothing will be. You've been acquired. You and your people now work for someone else. And even if that someone else likes you very much, it will have its own way of doing things. HR will have a new way of appraising people. Finance will have a new way of formatting the numbers. And so on; there will be new processes, policies, and procedures galore.

And so, to answer your question, the quickest and most appropriate way for you to adjust is: buy in. You don't have to stifle yourself. But your energy about change should be positive and any criticisms constructive. No "but we used to . . ." and "it was better in the old days" moaning and groaning. Very bluntly, you gave that "right" away with the cash-out.

We realize that being acquired is one of the most traumatic upheavals a company can live through. For you personally, money may have taken any sting out. But if you want your people and organization to thrive, as clearly you do, then your message has to be simple. The past is over—embrace the new.

■   ■   ■

66

BRINGING THE OUTSIDE IN

I am a twenty-nine-year-old biochemist who works in a small company founded by my father thirty-two years ago. We haven't grown for some time, and I worry we could disappear altogether. My father and I have no management experience and can't seem to make our dreams come true. Will it help if I get an MBA or update my technical knowledge?

—VITÓRIA, BRAZIL

Unlikely. Your problem is too big and time is too short. Instead, you need to accept that you have reached a moment of truth in the evolution of many start-up and family-run ventures. A unique technology or product, plus passion and momentum, can take you only so far. Now you need help—from the outside.

Don't panic. Get out there and find a star CEO. Yes, that step can be anathema for owners and entrepreneurs in your situation, but it usually hurts only at the begin-

ning, as you hammer out new roles and relationships.
After that, it can be all upside, as outsiders, with their
experience and hunger for change, find the route to the
growth that has eluded you.

And you, incidentally, are in a particularly fortunate
position. The star you need could come from your own
industry. Big Pharma is having its own growth problems. And because of that, there are lots of talented executives who would likely jump at the chance to transform
a floundering family-operated biotech company.

Of course, to attract such a change agent, you will need
to give something up. You and your father, for instance,
may have to let go of daily operations, hiring, and strategic planning. You will also have to let go of some equity.
You simply cannot reel in a great outside CEO without
giving him or her a piece of the action. The good news is,
if your new star does the job well, you all win, financially
and otherwise, as the company grows and thrives.

Yes, letting go can be scary. But there's really nothing
to fear, since you and your father will retain majority
control of the company. Just be sure to use that control
judiciously.

Remember, you hired the star not to obey you—but
to save you!

■   ■   ■

WINNING AND LOSING

▪ *On Why Business Is Good* ▪

Winning could not have been published at a more fraught moment in the life cycle of world business. The technology bubble had burst, sapping enormous confidence from the system; the emergence of terrorism had introduced a new and seemingly intractable shakiness to the markets; and corporate scandals were in high gear. After more than a decade of exuberant go-go-go for business, suddenly there was a widespread sense of no-no-no. No growth, no certainty, no pride.

The last of these—the contention that business is inherently bad—has always struck us the most off base and, indeed, even the most dangerous to the future of a healthy society.

In this final set of answers, we explain why.

67

THE WAGES OF SOX

Has the new regulatory environment in the United States—brought on by its spate of corporate scandals—crippled the country's entrepreneurial spirit and dulled its competitive edge?

—NEW YORK, NEW YORK

No—but we have to be careful going forward.

Look, there can be no denying that in 2001, two major events significantly impacted the U.S. business environment. First, the well-publicized spate of corporate scandals that began to unfold that year led to the eventual passage of the Sarbanes-Oxley Act, with its new legion of constrictive financial reporting requirements and correspondingly severe penalties. SOX, as the act is commonly called, cast a real chill on risk taking. And while its requirements affected every company, small entrepreneurial ventures, with their limited staffs and tight cash flow, certainly felt its additional costs the most.

Second, there was 9/11, which sparked tough new immigration rules. While completely understandable, those rules happened to affect a visa provision called H-1B, which makes it harder for skilled foreign workers, i.e., future entrepreneurs, to stay in the United States after they complete their education.

Both SOX and H-1B had unintended consequences that could have really weakened American entrepreneurship. But they haven't. Here's why.

Take SOX to start. Without doubt, SOX was necessary. Investors desperately needed to see that the U.S. government was committed to keeping American business clean and fair. SOX did that, and that was great. But any law that passes the U.S. Senate by a vote of 99–0 *has* to be excessive—and SOX was.

Already, however, we have begun to see the most constrictive black-and-white strictures of SOX give way to good judgment by regulators. The SEC has very thoughtfully reevaluated and revised sections of SOX. Normalcy and equilibrium are creeping back into the system.

As for the new immigration laws, the picture isn't yet so positive. In 2004, in fact, the U.S. government cut the number of H-1B aliens permitted into the country by two-thirds—from 195,000 to 65,000—although the cost of sponsoring such aliens was reduced for employers. During our recent visits to dozens of American business schools, we heard about the difficulties wrought by this rule again and again, and not just from the young people themselves, but from the professors who want to help them achieve their dreams of building businesses in America.

That said, SOX is a good example of how a much-needed but overreaching law in the U.S. system can be modified to reflect marketplace realities, and it's likely the same will happen in regard to immigration. America was built in large part on the brains, heart, and sweat of newcomers, and it must continue to benefit from the future's best and brightest flowing through its doors from every corner of the world.

But even if the return to more open immigration rules is slow, America still has three huge competitive advantages in the global marketplace.

First, its government and its people are ardently pro-business. They believe in capitalism, and every aspect of the political system bolsters that belief. Taxes, while significant, are not onerous. Calls for protectionist measures are beaten down in favor of free-trade initiatives.

Second, the U.S. culture celebrates entrepreneurs.

Some of its biggest heroes include great inventors from Thomas Edison and Henry Ford to Bill Gates and Michael Dell. And there is absolutely no shame in telling people—including your parents—"I'm starting a business in the garage." In fact, it is more likely to cause envy or awe than dismay.

Third and finally, the United States has vast capital markets and the ingenuity to use them to build great enterprises. Europe, Japan, and Latin America lag far behind the United States in the capital or desire, or both, to pour resources into the venture funds that galvanize start-ups in every industry. Likewise, they lack the proliferation of private equity firms you find in the United States, with their penchant for turning business laggards into fiercely competitive organizations.

In the United States, good ideas and the entrepreneurs who spawn them don't go begging. Instead, they get pursued to the point that there is often more money than good ideas to invest it in.

Very simply, it's an entrepreneur's playground in America, and even excessive knee-jerk regulation cannot take the fun, energy, power—or spirit—out of it.

■　■　■

68

THE COCKTAIL PARTY CONSPIRACY THEORY

Do you believe that large corporations are riddled with office politics—the "who you know, not what you know" syndrome—such that many people are stifled in favor of those who posture in the right way?

—BILLERICAY, ESSEX, ENGLAND

There will always be office politics, but it goes too far to think that big business is "riddled" with it. Plenty of companies all over the world—winning companies—do everything in their power to get rid of it every day. In fact, they're *desperate* to. Why? Because every manager with a brain in his or her head knows that you win when the best performers—not the people who "posture in the right way"—get heard and get ahead. You don't think Microsoft grew into the most successful computer company in the world with a bunch of sycophantic dopes on the senior management team, do you? Or that Procter & Gamble reinvigorated its approach to innovation because it promoted a bunch of empty-headed rear-end kissers? No way. These companies, and thousands upon thousands like them, deliver results because they are meritocracies, where brains and sweat matter more than who had cocktails with the boss last week.

Office politics, in our experience, is mainly the province of just three types of employees. The first is boss haters. These are the perpetually disaffected individuals in most every organization who have a congenital disdain for authority. It's just part of their constitution. They go to work every day *looking* for palace intrigue, and part of that campaign is muttering away that some unworthy dunderhead got ahead because of "connections." The second type is underperformers, who use office politics to explain away their own shortcomings. They deserved the promotion, but Mary got it because she went to school with the boss's brother, and that kind of thing. And the third type is people who are underutilized—the bored. As the old saying goes, "Idle hands are the devil's workshop." Idle brains too.

Given the people behind office politics, it is easy to see why it mainly affects lousy companies. Good companies work ardently to root these types of people out, or to get them back on course. That doesn't mean they succeed completely, but they never stop trying.

■   ■   ■

69

WHAT TO TELL THE GRANDCHILDREN

After a successful and satisfying career as an engineer and manager, I am getting to the point where my grandchildren are turning to me for advice about educational and career paths for themselves. If you were in my shoes, what would you tell them?

—MILWAUKEE, WISCONSIN

Whenever we get this question, a strong image comes to mind. It's of a friend of ours who was encouraged (she would say, "shoved") by her parents—back in the 1970s—to become a doctor. At the time, getting a medical degree was like winning the lottery, but with a lot more respect attached. So, our friend went along with the plan. Her parents cheered; she soldiered on.

Fast-forward to the present. Our friend is taking photographs for a living—joyfully, we might add. She ditched her twenty-year career as a neurologist at age forty-five with the words "Life is too short to spend every day doing something you don't love."

That's what we would advise you to tell your grand-children.

Now, we realize that every era has its next big thing. In the 1970s, college kids were pressed to study geology, to capitalize on the growing number of opportunities in oil and gas exploration. In the '80s, investment banking and consulting were the gold mines of the future, and in the '90s, the collective mantra was, "Go Internet, young man." All in all, not bad stuff. The oil and gas industries continue to flourish. Investment banking and consulting continue to expand, making a lot of people fortunes. And the Internet, after enduring a period of bust, is strong and getting stronger.

Today, all arrows point toward the biotech, nanotech, and information technology industries, and the conver-gence among them. That's where the growth and great-est excitement will likely be over the next decades.

But that data matters only if your grandchildren hap-pen to like science or technology so much that they just can't learn enough about either or both.

If they don't, they should follow our friend's well-earned counsel: the only career worth pursuing is the one that turns your crank.

So, by all means, mention the next big thing to your

grandkids, but tell them with more gusto that they should do what they love. Tell them to grab on to the career that engages their brain and heart and soul and gives them meaning. Tell them that eventually, the money will come, and if it doesn't, in time, they will find themselves rich with something money can't buy.

And that, obviously, would be happiness.

■   ■   ■

70

GOOD-BYE, GENGHIS KHAN

"It is not sufficient that I succeed. Everyone else must fail" is a line attributed to Genghis Khan and sometimes quoted by the moguls of our own era. In the cutthroat, hypercompetitive business world today, what is your take on this attitude?

—STILLWATER, OKLAHOMA

It's nonsense, of course, because it's just not the way business usually works, nor should it be.

Now, obviously you're not going to sit around wishing your competitors well. All tough-minded businesspeople want to win—they want the most sales, the biggest market share, the highest profit margins, and so on.

But tough-minded businesspeople also realize that competitors, for all their aggravation, serve a purpose. They sharpen your focus. They keep you fierce and hungry. And the best of them raise the bar on every aspect of performance, from innovation to delivery.

Without competition, companies usually get fat and lazy. Case in point: all the bureaucratic monopolies out there that have foundered, largely due to the self-satisfaction and arrogance that came with achieving the very success they were after.

So, look, you may not want your competitors to win, but unlike Genghis, you want them around. It's good for customers, it's good for you (albeit sometimes painful), and it's good for business overall.

Now, taking the quote to the individual level—again, wrong, even for the most ambitious among us. We're not going to deny that schadenfreude exists; it's human nature to feel a small twinge of relief (or worse, happiness) when a colleague screws up. But the most successful people fight that instinct with everything in them. They know that someone else's candle going out, as the old saying goes, doesn't make their candle burn any brighter. It just makes the whole room darker.

The best thing that can happen at work—and in life—is to be surrounded by people who are smart and good. As with tough competitors, you learn from them and improve because of them. When they do well, so do you, either by their example or by being part of their team.

So maybe Mr. Khan was onto something eight hundred years ago, fighting other warlords on the Mongolian plain, but in today's world, mogul or not, his advice seems ready to retire.

■   ■   ■

71

AND THE LOSERS ARE . . .

All this talk about winning makes me wonder, is there any place for losers in this world? Only a small percentage of people succeed; what should all the nonwinners do, just kill themselves?

—BANGALORE, INDIA

What a question! It has to mean you see winning in purely economic terms. That's just not how it has to be.

We think about winning another way—as setting personal goals and achieving them, and (as important) enjoying the experience on the way. Winning has nothing—or everything—to do with your job. Yes, you can win as a corporate executive, but you can win just as meaningfully as a carpenter, math teacher, or singer in a wedding band. You can win raising a family, caring for your parents, or being a good friend—as long as those are the dreams you picked for yourself. Indeed, the biggest winners in the world are those who answer yes to the question, "Am I living the life I choose?"

One of the biggest winners we know is a person who by your economic definition would probably not qualify at all. Jim O'Connell graduated from Harvard Medical School. But instead of pursuing a prestigious and lucrative career, he has spent the past twenty-two years driving a van around Boston practically every night, delivering medical care to the homeless. He lives simply; money doesn't matter to him. And yet Jim's life is full of joy, and he is beloved by everyone lucky enough to know him, from street people to senators.

Look, winning and losing can't be quantified. They are states of mind, and losing happens only when you give up. Seen that way, then, the world can be filled with winners, and there is room for them all.

■   ■   ■

72

WHAT'S RIGHT ABOUT WAL-MART

Is Wal-Mart a force for good or evil in the world?

—EXETER, NEW HAMPSHIRE

We have heard this question increasingly in recent months, but perhaps with the most fervor by the high school student who posed it the way you see it here, with the added remark, "You claim business is good for society—but Wal-Mart destroys it."

Destroys it? No way.

Look, Wal-Mart is a great company. Maybe that's politically incorrect to say today, but it's absolutely true. Wal-Mart helps individuals, communities, and whole economies prosper.

Yes, Wal-Mart is huge and getting more so. Yes, its business model is threatening to competitors, and its purchasing power frightening to suppliers. But all that doesn't make Wal-Mart *bad*. It just makes Wal-Mart a big fat target for critics who, for reasons of their own, won't acknowledge the many ways Wal-Mart improves lives.

Take individuals. First and most obviously, Wal-Mart's prices have a massive positive impact on the quality of life of millions of consumers. No other retailer offers so many good products for so little, from groceries, to school supplies, to medicine, to home furnishings. And in doing so, Wal-Mart helps keep household expenses low in a way that no social or government program could even attempt.

In addition, Wal-Mart helps individuals in a more long-term and exciting way. It provides its employees with tremendous access to upward mobility, even those with modest educational credentials. The organization is filled with stories of employees who started on the floor or as cashiers and worked their way up to management positions. And with Wal-Mart's international growth, you are now seeing career paths that can start in merchandising in Texas, move to logistics in Arkansas, and end up in divisional leadership positions in Europe and Asia. Only the military comes close to Wal-Mart when it comes to providing training and opportunity for individuals who have no other way to break out of a paycheck-to-paycheck lifestyle and into a whole new world of possibility.

Wal-Mart's low prices and its large workforce, of

course, have a cumulative effect on the local and national economies where the company operates. Low prices keep inflation down, while the employees' purchasing power keeps demand high.

This is evil?

Now, there are critics who assert that Wal-Mart undermines America's economy by making it impossible for small businesses to get off the ground, let alone survive. But that claim just doesn't make sense. As a competitor, Wal-Mart really goes nowhere near the technology start-ups that are the lifeblood of the American economy—the burgeoning little technology ventures in Silicon Valley, the futuristic biotech labs in Boston and California, the innovative Internet "plays" popping up everywhere. As for more traditional start-ups—the kinds making products—if anything, they can be helped by Wal-Mart, which has shown it will give a chance to entrepreneurs gutsy enough to play their game. We know, for instance, of a Miami businesswoman, Tam Tran, who bootstrapped Anise Cosmetics, a nail polish and treatment company, but was able to jumpstart it into a national success *because* Wal-Mart had the resources and insight to take a chance on her unique product line. Two executives from the company helped Tam formulate a new marketing message and improve her packaging before launching her products in 1,400 Wal-Mart stores. "They were creative and proactive with me," she wrote us not long ago. "No other retailer took the time to even consider us. They were fair and most professional."

OK, so maybe Wal-Mart doesn't annihilate entrepreneurs. But as other critics claim, what about communities? Doesn't Wal-Mart wipe out mom-and-pop stores—the little pharmacies, hardware, furniture, and grocery stores—which took much better care of customers and employees?

Alas, this line of thinking is a case of nostalgia for a time that never was.

Yes, Wal-Mart has meant the end of many local stores, and yes, at some of them, customers might have been greeted by name when they walked in the door. But it was these same customers who *chose* to shop at Wal-Mart when it came to town, because low prices, apparently, meant more to their quality of life than a wave and a smile. No conspiracy; just the free market at work.

As for better-cared-for employees—nonsense. In most small towns, the store owner was the one who drove the best car, lived in the fanciest house, and belonged to the local country club. Meanwhile, his employees weren't exactly sharing the wealth. They rarely had life insurance or health benefits, and they certainly did not receive much in the way of training or big salaries. And few of these store owners had plans for growth or expansion;

their lives were pretty nicely set. That was good for them but a killer for any employees seeking life-changing careers.

Critics also lambaste Wal-Mart for being brutal to its suppliers. It's hard to negotiate, they say, with the company that "owns" the channel. Be it swing sets or beef jerky, you sell to Wal-Mart on its terms, or you don't sell at all.

We'd say this is pretty true. Wal-Mart's huge market share gives it substantial leverage over its suppliers. But in decades of negotiating with them at General Electric, for example, Wal-Mart buyers were never unethical or unfair. They were just tough. GE won plenty of negotiations with Wal-Mart and lost a few. But losing had its upside. It forced GE to look inside itself to see how it could do *its* job better—to lower its manufacturing costs, for instance, or to be more flexible in how a product was designed or packaged.

Ultimately, prices stayed low and the customer won. And that is what drives Wal-Mart—keeping its customers satisfied—and why it keeps increasing its sales and profits.

Yes, there will be casualties because of Wal-Mart's success. Some competitors will certainly fold to its business model, and some jobs will be lost in the process. But in that way, Wal-Mart is no different from Toyota in the automotive industry. When Toyota arrived in the 1970s, it too was accused of upsetting the status quo. Decades have passed, and most people now accept that Toyota simply had a better way of doing business. Its value proposition to consumers raised the standards of the entire industry, requiring many car companies that had lost their manufacturing and design edge to wake up, reinvent their ways, and start making better cars for a lot less.

Toyota was a change agent, and as such, has done more for society than any failing company.

And that's the Wal-Mart story too. It's a great company that helps consumers and employees win and grow, and as long as it does, it will too—deservedly so.

■   ■   ■

73

THE REAL VERDICT ON BUSINESS

In the days and weeks after the Enron verdicts were handed down in May 2006, there was an understandable focus on the victims of the company's collapse: employees who lost their jobs and pensions, shareholders who collectively lost billions of dollars, and residents of Houston, where Enron played a large charitable role.

These victims, it was said, could take only cold comfort in the verdicts. Yes, the system worked. In fact, the old system worked, since Jeff Skilling and Ken Lay were tried under laws that were on the books long before the passage of the Sarbanes-Oxley Act in 2002. But the convictions, everyone rightly agreed, could not bring back all that lost money or repair all those disrupted lives.

Nor, we would add, do they seem likely to bring back the optimism, confidence, and courage that made business so much fun.

Yes, fun. Remember? Before business-writ-large became demonized by Enron and other companies where wrongdoing was found, being in business felt different. The bursting of the dot-com bubble certainly had an impact, but we're talking about a phenomenon that supersedes that. It's hard to quantify, but we sense a kind of fear and trembling everywhere we go. People worry about taking risks. They're anxious about the future. They're hesitant to say they love work. In short, business has lost some of its spark. What an unnecessary shame.

Why? Because if there is one thing the corporate scandals have shown us, it's that bad behavior is actually pretty rare. The *Wall Street Journal* estimates that about one thousand people have been convicted of corporate crimes since July 2002. That's one thousand—not ten thousand or even a hundred thousand—out of the tens of millions of businesspeople. Not every case of bad behavior has been uncovered, but an overwhelming number of businesses play by the rules, and most of the time, the rules work.

We know that, and you probably do too. You just might be having a hard time admitting it these days. Some time ago, we were speaking to a group of insurance agents in Florida. They were a cheerful bunch until one man asked: "Is it just me, or do other people here feel ashamed to admit they work in business now? I mean, sort of . . . dirty? I know I haven't done anything wrong

and that I work with good people. But still . . ." There
was silence, and then the crowd gave him a round of
supportive applause. They were all in the tank together.

This sort of self-loathing isn't the only worrisome
fallout of the changed business climate. Managers everywhere tell us that they are spending vast quantities
of time in defensive mode, heads down, chanting, "Compliance, compliance, compliance." Now, we're obviously for accuracy in reporting—and ironclad integrity.
But the blood in the water, even five years after Enron,
has too many businesses swimming in circles instead of
charting new horizons.

Look, business isn't perfect, and it never will be, as
long as it is comprised of human beings. After all, we have
laws galore, and people still drive above the speed limit,
rob convenience stores, and of course, do far worse. The
FBI raids one congressman's office; another is indicted
and resigns. A journalist at a respected newspaper fab-
ricates stories for years. A man of the cloth takes what's
in the collection plate to fund a lavish lifestyle. Just as
you could write off business because of such aberrations
as Enron, you could write off all public servants, the
media, and the clergy because a minute percentage of
politicians, journalists, or padres. But you might as well
write off all of humanity.

Business is a huge source of vitality in the world and

a noble enterprise. Thriving, decent companies are everywhere, and they should be celebrated. They create
jobs and opportunities, provide revenue for government,
and are the foundation of a free and democratic society.
People who work at winning companies give back: they
pay taxes, mentor in schools, volunteer at firehouses. So,
don't buy the line that Enron is business, and business is
bad. Enron and the others were exceptions. Business is
good. In fact, business is great.

Yes, Enron had its victims. The whole awful story
is a tragedy. But we can't let a relatively small group
of companies rewrite reality and make businesspeople cower in shame and lose their courage. We can't let
business—society's engine and great hope—be Enron's
final victim.

■   ■   ■

74

WHAT DO YOU CALL WINNING?

Early in my career, I heard it said, "There is no profit in winning in the world if you lose your soul." I wonder now if that is true—if future historians will look back to our times and say, "They won personal fortunes in a new global economy, but they destroyed families, communities, and even nations." My question to you then is: what do you call winning? Isn't it about something more than the markets can offer?

—EDINBURGH, SCOTLAND

Winning, actually, doesn't have anything to do with the markets. Or we should say, it doesn't *have* to have anything to do with them. By our definition, winning is a personal journey. It's about you as an individual setting a goal and achieving it. That goal could be creating and supporting a happy, healthy family. It could be founding or funding a homeless shelter. It could be teaching children to read; it could be sailing around the world.

And then again, it could be building a thriving company that succeeds in the global marketplace.

Winning is about reaching the destination you choose. It is not necessarily about profit, although it can be. But winning is, at its most fundamental, about making something of your life. It is about progress and meaning. It is about achievement.

Winning is not about destroying families, communities, and nations. Not even when the winning is done by companies taking part in the new global economy. In fact, your suggestion that economic success is somehow, by definition, morally corrupt is just dead wrong.

Look, winning in business is not a zero-sum game. In sports, when one team wins, the other loses. On the other hand, in business, when a company wins, there are usually lots of collateral winners too. A successful company's executives and shareholders benefit, of course, but so do its employees, distributors, and suppliers. In some cases—Microsoft and Amgen are two good examples out of thousands—a company's success has led to the creation of dozens of more companies, who supply or sell to the parent company. Sometimes they create whole new industries, with slews of new competitors. The most important thing is that all these new companies create jobs, the lifeblood of any society. When people have meaningful work, they have the freedom to set their own goals, not just survive. They can educate their children, travel, or give to charity. They can dream.

Along with creating jobs, winning companies pay taxes, as do their employees, funding countless programs, from schools to hospitals and courts.

What in all of this "destroys"?

Now, obviously, there are people in business who lose their souls to profit, as you put it. It's an old story that, very unfortunately, gets regularly refreshed with some new account of corporate lying, cheating, or stealing. There are and always will be corrupt jerks out there, and not just in business, but in every field, from the priesthood to politics.

But we strongly believe that most people in business, just like people in general, are good. They want to win the right way, cleanly, fairly, and by the rules. They want to start companies or help build them. They want to search every day for new ideas. They want to invent new technologies and ways of getting things done. They want a different future—a better one for themselves, their families, friends, and colleagues.

Will future historians look back on these people and say their definition of winning ruined the world?

Or might they say they made it a better place?

■   ■   ■

THE BOOK THAT STARTED IT ALL

WINNING

ISBN 0-06-075394-3 (hardcover)

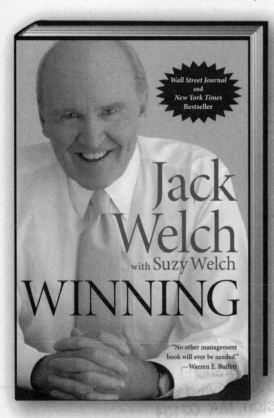

Wall Street Journal and New York Times Bestseller

Jack Welch with Suzy Welch

WINNING

"No other management book will ever be needed."
—Warren E. Buffett

"Jack Welch is back with a far-reaching book on all things business."
—*Fast Company*

"When you talk with Jack about management, his energy and passion fill the room. You get a similar experience with this book—the same qualities jump at you from every page."
—Warren E. Buffett, chairman, Berkshire Hathaway

"A candid and comprehensive look at how to succeed in business—for everyone from college graduates to CEOs."
—Bill Gates, chairman, Microsoft Corporation

⊙ **Collins** An Imprint of HarperCollins Publishers www.harpercollins.com